Enrichment Studies Volume 1

A Year of Lesson Plans
for Art, Music, Literature, and More
(Grades 1–12)

by
Sonya Shafer

Enrichment Studies, Volume 1: A Year of Lesson Plans for Art, Music, Literature, and More

Cover Design: Sarah Shafer

ISBN 978-1-61634-301-9 printed
ISBN 978-1-61634-302-6 electronic download

Published by
Simply Charlotte Mason, LLC
930 New Hope Road #11-892
Lawrenceville, Georgia 30045
simplycharlottemason.com

Printed by PrintLogic, Inc.
Monroe, Georgia, USA

Contents

How to Use

This book of lesson plans contains resource suggestions and assignments to help you combine all of your students together to enjoy an enriching feast of subjects as a family. The feast includes:

- Picture Study
- Poetry
- Shakespeare
- Music Study
- Nature Study
- Hymn Study
- Scripture Memory
- Handicrafts
- Art Instruction
- Habit Training
- Foreign Language
- Literature (Family Read-Aloud)

Complete one lesson per day to finish these studies in a school year. The weekly schedule each Term details how your family can enjoy this wonderful variety of studies in just one hour per day.

The Charlotte Mason methods you will use with this book are explained on page 129.

Complete Year's Resources List

- Book of Centuries (one per family and older student)
- *Creating a Masterpiece*: Pastels video(s) of choice and materials
- *Enjoy the Poems of Robert Louis Stevenson*
- *Handicrafts Made Simple: Crochet* DVD and materials
- *Handicrafts Made Simple: Hand Sewing* DVD and materials
- *Journaling a Year in Nature* (one per person), pencils, watercolor paints, field guides
- *Laying Down the Rails for Children*
- *Music Study with the Masters: J. S. Bach*
- *Music Study with the Masters: Beethoven*
- *Music Study with the Masters: Chopin*
- *Picture Study Portfolio: Constable*
- *Picture Study Portfolio: Rembrandt*
- *Picture Study Portfolio: Velazquez*
- Scripture Memory Verse Pack 1
- *Shakespeare in Three Steps: A Midsummer Night's Dream* with (optional) *The Arkangel Shakespeare* audio recording
- *Singing the Great Hymns*
- *Speaking [Spanish] with Miss Mason and Francois* (Select your preferred language.)

plus Family Read-Aloud Books (*Select one group.)

Young Group

- *The Trumpet of the Swan* by E. B. White
- *All-of-a-Kind Family* by Sydney Taylor
- *The Complete Tales of Winnie-the-Pooh* by A. A. Milne (contains both *Winnie-the-Pooh* and *The House at Pooh Corner*)
- *Five Little Peppers and How They Grew* by Margaret Sidney
- *The Wonderful Wizard of Oz* by L. Frank Baum
- *Mr. Popper's Penguins* by Richard Atwater
- *Pinocchio* by Carlo Collodi

Middle Group

- *The Pilgrim's Progress* by John Bunyan
- *Bambi: A Life in the Woods* by Felix Salten
- *The Story of the Treasure Seekers* by E. Nesbit
- *The Swiss Family Robinson* by Johann Wyss
- *My Side of the Mountain* by Jean Craighead George
- *Treasure Island* by Robert Louis Stevenson

Older Group

- *The Hobbit* by J. R. R. Tolkien
- *The Fellowship of the Ring* by J. R. R. Tolkien
- *The Two Towers* by J. R. R. Tolkien
- *The Return of the King* by J. R. R. Tolkien

- *Where the Red Fern Grows* by Wilson Rawls
- *The Innocence of Father Brown* by G. K. Chesterton

* Three options are given for Family Read-Aloud books: a group of books for younger students, a group for middle students, and a group for older students. Select one of the groups to read aloud to your family—the one that best reflects the age range of most of your students. The Young Selection is geared toward approximately grades 1–4, Middle Selection for grades 5–8, and Older Selection for grades 9–12. If you have a wide range of student ages to accommodate, you may want to select one group of books to read aloud and assign another group to older students to read independently.

Suggestions for Where to Find the Resources

Simply Charlotte Mason
- Book of Centuries (one per family and older student)
- *Enjoy the Poems of Robert Louis Stevenson*
- *Handicrafts Made Simple: Crochet* DVD
- *Handicrafts Made Simple: Hand Sewing* DVD
- *Journaling a Year in Nature* (one per person)
- *Laying Down the Rails for Children*
- *Music Study with the Masters: J. S. Bach*
- *Music Study with the Masters: Beethoven*
- *Music Study with the Masters: Chopin*
- *Picture Study Portfolio: Constable*
- *Picture Study Portfolio: Rembrandt*
- *Picture Study Portfolio: Velazquez*
- Scripture Memory Verse Pack 1
- *Shakespeare in Three Steps: A Midsummer Night's Dream* (and optional *The Arkangel Shakespeare* audio dramatization recording)
- *Singing the Great Hymns*

Cherrydale Press
(Select your preferred foreign language at cherrydalepress.com.)
- *Speaking [Spanish] with Miss Mason and Francois*

Creating a Masterpiece
(Access their video library at creatingamasterpiece.com.)
- *Creating a Masterpiece*: Pastels video(s)

Public Domain
(You can probably download these books for free at http://gutenberg.org, http://books.google.com, or http://archive.org.)
- *Bambi: A Life in the Woods* by Felix Salten (Middle Group)
- *Five Little Peppers and How They Grew* by Margaret Sidney (Young Group)
- *The Innocence of Father Brown* by G. K. Chesterton (Older Group)
- *The Pilgrim's Progress* by John Bunyan (Middle Group)
- *Pinocchio* by Carlo Collodi (Young Group)
- *The Story of the Treasure Seekers* by E. Nesbit (Middle Group)
- *The Swiss Family Robinson* by Johann Wyss (Middle Group)
- *Treasure Island* by Robert Louis Stevenson (Middle Group)
- *The Wonderful Wizard of Oz* by L. Frank Baum (Young Group)

Your Local Library or Favorite Book Store
- *All-of-a-Kind Family* by Sydney Taylor (Young Group)
- *The Complete Tales of Winnie-the-Pooh* by A. A. Milne (contains both *Winnie-the-Pooh* and *The House at Pooh Corner*) (Young Group)
- *The Fellowship of the Ring* by J. R. R. Tolkien (Older Group)

- *The Hobbit* by J. R. R. Tolkien (Older Group)
- *Mr. Popper's Penguins* by Richard Atwater (Young Group)
- *My Side of the Mountain* by Jean Craighead George (Middle Group)
- *The Return of the King* by J. R. R. Tolkien (Older Group)
- *The Trumpet of the Swan* by E. B. White (Young Group)
- *The Two Towers* by J. R. R. Tolkien (Older Group)
- *Where the Red Fern Grows* by Wilson Rawls (Older Group)

Term 1

(12 weeks; 5 lessons/week)

Term 1 Resource List

- Scripture Memory Verse Pack 1
- Book of Centuries (one per family and older student)
- *Handicrafts Made Simple: Hand Sewing*
- *Picture Study Portfolio: Rembrandt*
- *Enjoy the Poems of Robert Louis Stevenson*
- *Music Study with the Masters: J. S. Bach*
- *Journaling a Year in Nature* (one per person), pencils, watercolor paints, field guides
- *Singing the Great Hymns*
- *Speaking [Spanish] with Miss Mason and Francois* (or your preferred language)
- *Laying Down the Rails for Children*

Plus Family Read-Aloud Books (Select one group.)

Young Group

- *The Trumpet of the Swan*
- *All-of-a-Kind Family*
- *The Complete Tales of Winnie-the-Pooh*

Middle Group

- *The Pilgrim's Progress*
- *Bambi: A Life in the Woods*
- *The Story of the Treasure Seekers*

Older Group

- *The Hobbit*
- *The Fellowship of the Ring*

Suggested Weekly Schedule

Day 1 *(approx. 1 hour)*	Day 2 *(approx. 1 hour)*	Day 3 *(approx. 1 hour)*	Day 4 *(approx. 1 hour)*	Day 5 *(approx. 1+ hour)*
• Scripture Memory (10 min.) • Habits (10 min.) • Picture Study (10 min.) • Family Read-Aloud (20 min.)	• Scripture Memory (10 min.) • Hymn Study (5 min.) • Poetry (5 min.) • Foreign Language (15 min.) • Family Read-Aloud (20 min.)	• Scripture Memory (10 min.) • Habits (10 min.) • Music Study (10 min.) • Family Read-Aloud (20 min.)	• Scripture Memory (10 min.) • Hymn Study (5 min.) • Foreign Language (15 min.) • Handicrafts (20 min.) • Family Read-Aloud (20 min.)	• Scripture Memory (10 min.) • Nature Study (15+ min.) • Repetition: Poem (5 min.) • Family Read-Aloud (20 min.)

Lesson 1

Materials Needed
- Verse Pack 1
- *Laying Down the Rails for Children*
- *Picture Study Portfolio: Rembrandt*
- *The Trumpet of the Swan* OR *The Pilgrim's Progress* OR *The Hobbit*

Scripture Memory: Work on learning a passage from Verse Pack 1 and review previously memorized verses.

Tip: See page 129 for helpful notes on Scripture Memory, including a simple and effective way to review.

Habits: Select one habit from *Laying Down the Rails for Children* to focus on for the next six weeks. Read aloud one lesson from that habit in *Laying Down the Rails for Children.*

Tip: See page 129 for more on habit training.

Picture Study: Read together the first half of "The Story of Rembrandt" from *Picture Study Portfolio: Rembrandt,* page 11 and part of 12, and ask for an oral narration. Be sure to show the students the portrait of Rembrandt on the cover of the book.

Tip: See page 129 for an explanation of narration.

Family Read-Aloud: Select one family literature read-aloud book from the three options listed below, based on the age range of the students who will be listening, and read the pages indicated.
Young Selection: Read together *The Trumpet of the Swan*, chapter 1, "Sam."
Middle Selection: Read together *The Pilgrim's Progress*, "The Author's Apology for his Book."
Older Selection: Read together or assign as independent reading *The Hobbit*, the first half of chapter 1, "An Unexpected Party."

Lesson 2

Materials Needed
- Verse Pack 1
- *Singing the Great Hymns*
- *Enjoy the Poems of Robert Louis Stevenson*
- *Speaking [Spanish] with Miss Mason and Francois*
- *The Trumpet of the Swan* OR *The Pilgrim's Progress* OR *The Hobbit*

Book of Centuries Timeline

wk 1

Book of Centuries Timeline

Scripture Memory: Work on learning a passage from Verse Pack 1 and review previously memorized verses.

Hymn Study: Sing together all the stanzas of "I Sing the Mighty Power of God," pages 12 and 13 in *Singing the Great Hymns.*

Poetry: Read together "Summer Sun" from *Enjoy the Poems of Robert Louis Stevenson*, page 9.

Foreign Language: Work on a series from *Speaking [Spanish] with Miss Mason and Francois* (or your preferred language).

Family Read-Aloud: Continue reading your selection below.
Young Selection: Read together *The Trumpet of the Swan*, chapter 2, "The Pond."
Middle Selection: Read together *The Pilgrim's Progress*, from the beginning ("As I walked through the wilderness of this world") through Christian's encounter with Obstinate ("And I will go back to my place, said Obstinate; I will be no companion of such misled, fantastical fellows.").
Older Selection: Read together or assign as independent reading *The Hobbit*, the last half of chapter 1, "An Unexpected Party."

Tip: Feel free to do the different assignments at various times throughout the day. For example, you may want to do Scripture Memory at breakfast or save Poetry for a special treat at Tea Time or do your Family Read-Aloud at bedtime. Make your schedule your servant, not your master.

Lesson 3

Materials Needed

- Verse Pack 1
- *Laying Down the Rails for Children*
- *Music Study with the Masters: J. S. Bach*
- *The Trumpet of the Swan* OR *The Pilgrim's Progress* OR *The Hobbit*

Scripture Memory: Work on learning a passage from Verse Pack 1 and review previously memorized verses.

Habits: Read aloud one lesson from your selected habit in *Laying Down the Rails for Children.*

Music Study: Use the Listen and Learn notes on page 33 in the *Music Study with the Masters: J. S. Bach* book to help you listen to and discuss *Brandenburg Concerto No. 2 in F Major.*

Tip: You don't have to limit your listening to only scheduled Music Study times. Feel free to play the composer's music any time throughout the week. The more the students hear it, the more familiar it will become.

Book of Centuries Timeline

Family Read-Aloud: Continue reading your selection below.
Young Selection: Read together *The Trumpet of the Swan*, chapter 3, "A Visitor."
Middle Selection: Read together *The Pilgrim's Progress*, beginning where you left off last time through Pliable's return home ("And thus much concerning Pliable.").
Older Selection: Read together or assign as independent reading *The Hobbit*, the first half of chapter 2, "Roast Mutton."

Lesson 4

Materials Needed

- Verse Pack 1
- *Singing the Great Hymns*
- *Speaking [Spanish] with Miss Mason and Francois*
- *Handicrafts Made Simple: Hand Sewing* DVD and booklet
- *The Trumpet of the Swan* OR *The Pilgrim's Progress* OR *The Hobbit*

Scripture Memory: Work on learning a passage from Verse Pack 1 and review previously memorized verses.

Hymn Study: Sing together all the stanzas of "Like a River Glorious," pages 14 and 15 in *Singing the Great Hymns*.

Foreign Language: Work on a series from *Speaking [Spanish] with Miss Mason and Francois.*

Handicrafts: Watch session 1 of the *Handicrafts Made Simple: Hand Sewing* DVD and shop for supplies today or later this week.

Family Read-Aloud: Continue reading your selection below.
Young Selection: Read together *The Trumpet of the Swan*, chapter 4, "The Cygnets."
Middle Selection: Read together *The Pilgrim's Progress*, beginning where you left off last time through Christian's attempt at climbing the hill to Mr. Legality's house ("Here, therefore, he sweat and did quake for fear.")
Older Selection: Read together or assign as independent reading *The Hobbit*, the last half of chapter 2, "Roast Mutton."

Lesson 5

Materials Needed

- Verse Pack 1
- *Journaling a Year in Nature*, pencils, watercolor paints, field guides
- *Enjoy the Poems of Robert Louis Stevenson*
- *The Trumpet of the Swan* OR *The Pilgrim's Progress* OR *The Hobbit*

Scripture Memory: Work on learning a passage from Verse Pack 1 and review previously memorized verses.

Book of Centuries Timeline

Nature Study: Select and complete a nature study for this season from *Journaling a Year in Nature.*

Tip: Feel free to spend a good while outside. Charlotte Mason's students enjoyed a complete half-day in the fields every week. See page 129 for an explanation of nature study.

Poem Repetition: Read aloud the poem "My Shadow" from *Enjoy the Poems of Robert Louis Stevenson*, page 10, and explain that the students will be learning this poem over the next few weeks.

Tip: If you or your students would prefer to learn a different Stevenson poem, feel free to substitute one of your own selection.

Family Read-Aloud: Continue reading your selection below.
Young Selection: Read together *The Trumpet of the Swan*, chapter 5, "Louis."
Middle Selection: Read together *The Pilgrim's Progress*, beginning where you left off last time through Christian's arrival at the gate ("At last there came a grave person to the gate, named Good-will, who asked who was there? and whence he came? and what he would have?").
Older Selection: Read together or assign as independent reading *The Hobbit*, chapter 3, "A Short Rest."

Lesson 6

WK 1

Materials Needed

- Verse Pack 1
- *Laying Down the Rails for Children*
- *Picture Study Portfolio: Rembrandt*
- Book of Centuries
- *The Trumpet of the Swan* OR *The Pilgrim's Progress* OR *The Hobbit*

Scripture Memory: Work on learning a passage from Verse Pack 1 and review previously memorized verses.

Habits: Read aloud one lesson from your selected habit in *Laying Down the Rails for Children.*

Picture Study: Ask students what they remember from last time's reading about Rembrandt. Read the rest of "The Story of Rembrandt" from *Picture Study Portfolio: Rembrandt,* pages 12–14, and ask for an oral narration. Enter Rembrandt in your Book of Centuries.

Rembrandt van Ryn, artist (1606–1669)

Tip: See page 130 for an explanation of the Book of Centuries.

Family Read-Aloud: Continue reading your selection below.
Young Selection: Read together *The Trumpet of the Swan*, chapter 6, "Off to Montana."
Middle Selection: Read together *The Pilgrim's Progress*, beginning where you left off last time through Interpreter's explanation of 2 Corinthians 4:18 ("therefore it is, that the first of these so suddenly fall into amity, and that distance is so continued between the second.").
Older Selection: Read together or assign as independent reading *The Hobbit*, the first half of chapter 4, "Over Hill and Under Hill."

Book of Centuries Timeline

Lesson 7

Materials Needed
- Verse Pack 1
- *Singing the Great Hymns*
- *Enjoy the Poems of Robert Louis Stevenson*
- *Speaking [Spanish] with Miss Mason and Francois*
- *The Trumpet of the Swan* OR *The Pilgrim's Progress* OR *The Hobbit*

Scripture Memory: Work on learning a passage from Verse Pack 1 and review previously memorized verses.

Hymn Study: Sing together all the stanzas of "I Sing the Mighty Power of God," pages 12 and 13 in *Singing the Great Hymns.*

Poetry: Read together "My Shadow" from *Enjoy the Poems of Robert Louis Stevenson*, page 10.

Reminder: Make a copy of Enjoy the Poems of Robert Louis Stevenson, page 10, for every student who can read for lesson 10.

Foreign Language: Work on a series from *Speaking [Spanish] with Miss Mason and Francois.*

Family Read-Aloud: Continue reading your selection below.
Young Selection: Read together *The Trumpet of the Swan*, chapter 7, "School Days."
Middle Selection: Read together *The Pilgrim's Progress*, beginning where you left off last time through Christian's departure from Interpreter ("Wherefore they showed me were, and let me be Thankful, O good Interpreter, to thee.").
Older Selection: Read together or assign as independent reading *The Hobbit*, the last half of chapter 4, "Over Hill and Under Hill."

Tip: You may complete a lesson's assignments in any order that works best for your family's schedule and at any times of the day. Try to sequence lessons throughout the day to use different parts of the student's brain and body as you go along. In other words, don't schedule two "book-heavy"

Book of Centuries Timeline

assignments back to back. You might put hymn singing or oral foreign language in between reading assignments, for example.

Lesson 8

Materials Needed

- Verse Pack 1
- *Laying Down the Rails for Children*
- *Music Study with the Masters: J. S. Bach*
- *The Trumpet of the Swan* OR *The Pilgrim's Progress* OR *The Hobbit*

Scripture Memory: Work on learning a passage from Verse Pack 1 and review previously memorized verses.

Habits: Read aloud one lesson from your selected habit in *Laying Down the Rails for Children.*

Music Study: Use the Listen and Learn notes on page 34 in the *Music Study with the Masters: J. S. Bach* book to help you listen to *Cello Suite No. 1 in G Major* and have fun.

Tip: Don't worry about saving a particular music piece for the lesson in which it is scheduled to be discussed. It might be good for the students to hear a piece a few times before they learn more details about it.

Family Read-Aloud: Continue reading your selection below.
Young Selection: Read together *The Trumpet of the Swan*, chapter 8, "Love."
Middle Selection: Read together *The Pilgrim's Progress*, beginning where you left off last time through Christian's rest when he drops the roll ("And with that Christian started up, and sped him on his way, and went apace, till he came to the top of the hill.").
Older Selection: Read together or assign as independent reading *The Hobbit*, the first half of chapter 5, "Riddles in the Dark."

Lesson 9

Materials Needed

- Verse Pack 1
- *Singing the Great Hymns*
- *Speaking [Spanish] with Miss Mason and Francois*
- *Handicrafts Made Simple: Hand Sewing* DVD, booklet, and materials
- *The Trumpet of the Swan* OR *The Pilgrim's Progress* OR *The Hobbit*

Scripture Memory: Work on learning a passage from Verse Pack 1 and review previously memorized verses.

Hymn Study: Sing together all the stanzas of "Like a River Glorious," pages 14 and 15 in *Singing the Great Hymns.*

Foreign Language: Work on a series from *Speaking [Spanish] with Miss Mason and Francois.*

Handicrafts: Watch session 2 of the *Handicrafts Made Simple: Hand Sewing* DVD and practice the running stitch.

Family Read-Aloud: Continue reading your selection below.
Young Selection: Read together *The Trumpet of the Swan*, chapter 9, "The Trumpet."
Middle Selection: Read together *The Pilgrim's Progress*, beginning where you left off last time through Christian's telling Piety what he saw ("but now I thank God I am here, and I thank you for receiving of me.").
Older Selection: Read together or assign as independent reading *The Hobbit*, the last half of chapter 5, "Riddles in the Dark."

Lesson 10

Materials Needed

- Verse Pack 1
- *Journaling a Year in Nature*, pencils, watercolor paints, field guides
- *Enjoy the Poems of Robert Louis Stevenson*; copies of page 10
- *The Trumpet of the Swan* OR *The Pilgrim's Progress* OR *The Hobbit*

Scripture Memory: Work on learning a passage from Verse Pack 1 and review previously memorized verses.

Nature Study: Select and complete a nature study for this season from *Journaling a Year in Nature.*

Poem Repetition: Give each student who can read a copy of the poem "My Shadow" from *Enjoy the Poems of Robert Louis Stevenson*, page 10. Read it aloud as the students follow along on their printed copies. Encourage them to read through the poem on their own frequently during this term to help them learn it.

Tip: *Students who cannot yet read will most likely be able to learn the poem simply by hearing it read or recited during your Poem Repetition time each week. If you would like to, you may determine another time during the week to again read the poem aloud to your non-reading students, so they can hear it twice a week.*

Family Read-Aloud: Continue reading your selection below.
Young Selection: Read together *The Trumpet of the Swan*, chapter 10, "Money Trouble."
Middle Selection: Read together *The Pilgrim's Progress*, beginning where you

Book of Centuries Timeline

Book of Centuries Timeline

left off last time through Christian's song in the chamber of Peace ("And dwell already the next door to heaven!").
Older Selection: Read together or assign as independent reading *The Hobbit*, chapter 6, "Out of the Frying-Pan into the Fire."

Tip: Don't worry if you miss a day of a Family Read-Aloud along the way. You will have some extra days scheduled to catch up.

Lesson 11

Materials Needed

- Verse Pack 1
- *Laying Down the Rails for Children*
- *Picture Study Portfolio: Rembrandt*
- *The Trumpet of the Swan* OR *The Pilgrim's Progress* OR *The Hobbit*

Scripture Memory: Work on learning a passage from Verse Pack 1 and review previously memorized verses.

Habits: Read aloud one lesson from your selected habit in *Laying Down the Rails for Children.*

Be sure to take advantage of every opportunity to practice the habit your family is working on. It is the repetition that makes an action or an attitude a habit. The lessons in Laying Down the Rails for Children *are designed to help everyone focus on the habit at hand and be motivated to practice it as often as possible.*

Picture Study: Ask students what they recall from the story of Rembrandt. Do a picture study of *The Night Watch* from *Picture Study Portfolio: Rembrandt,* then discuss its Leading Thoughts on page 18 of the book.

Family Read-Aloud: Continue reading your selection below.
Young Selection: Read together *The Trumpet of the Swan*, chapter 11, "Camp Kookooskoos."
Middle Selection: Read together *The Pilgrim's Progress*, beginning where you left off last time through Christian's first sighting of Apollyon ("Therefore he resolved to venture and stand his ground; for, thought he, had I no more in mine eye than the saving of my life, it would be the best way to stand.").
Older Selection: Read together or assign as independent reading *The Hobbit*, the first half of chapter 7, "Queer Lodgings."

Lesson 12

Materials Needed

- Verse Pack 1

Book of Centuries Timeline

- *Singing the Great Hymns*
- *Enjoy the Poems of Robert Louis Stevenson*
- *Speaking [Spanish] with Miss Mason and Francois*
- *The Trumpet of the Swan* OR *The Pilgrim's Progress* OR *The Hobbit*

Scripture Memory: Work on learning a passage from Verse Pack 1 and review previously memorized verses.

Hymn Study: Sing together all the stanzas of "I Sing the Mighty Power of God," pages 12 and 13 in *Singing the Great Hymns.*

Poetry: Ask students what they recall from the two poems you've read so far by Robert Louis Stevenson. Read together the short biography on pages 7 and 8 of *Enjoy the Poems of Robert Louis Stevenson* and ask for an oral narration. Be sure to show students the picture of Stevenson on the first page of the book.

Foreign Language: Work on a series from *Speaking [Spanish] with Miss Mason and Francois.*

Family Read-Aloud: Continue reading your selection below.
Young Selection: Read together *The Trumpet of the Swan*, chapter 12, "A Rescue."
Middle Selection: Read together *The Pilgrim's Progress*, beginning where you left off last time through Christian's recovery from his battle with Apollyon ("But he met with no other affront from Apollyon quite through this valley.").
Older Selection: Read together or assign as independent reading *The Hobbit*, the last half of chapter 7, "Queer Lodgings."

Lesson 13

Materials Needed

- Verse Pack 1
- *Laying Down the Rails for Children*
- *Music Study with the Masters: J. S. Bach*
- *The Trumpet of the Swan* OR *The Pilgrim's Progress* OR *The Hobbit*

Scripture Memory: Work on learning a passage from Verse Pack 1 and review previously memorized verses.

Habits: Read aloud one lesson from your selected habit in *Laying Down the Rails for Children.*

Music Study: Use the Listen and Learn notes on page 35 in the *Music Study with the Masters: J. S. Bach* book to help you listen to and discuss *Concerto for 2 Violins in D Minor.*

Family Read-Aloud: Continue reading your selection below.
Young Selection: Read together *The Trumpet of the Swan*, chapter 13, "End of Summer."
Middle Selection: Read together *The Pilgrim's Progress*, beginning where you left off last time through Christian's song at coming through the Valley of the

Book of Centuries Timeline

Shadow ("Might have been catch'd, entangled, and cast down; But since I live, let Jesus wear the crown.").
Older Selection: Read together or assign as independent reading *The Hobbit*, the first half of chapter 8, "Flies and Spiders."

Lesson 14

Materials Needed

- Verse Pack 1
- *Singing the Great Hymns*
- *Speaking [Spanish] with Miss Mason and Francois*
- *Handicrafts Made Simple: Hand Sewing* DVD, booklet, and materials
- *The Trumpet of the Swan* OR *The Pilgrim's Progress* OR *The Hobbit*

Scripture Memory: Work on learning a passage from Verse Pack 1 and review previously memorized verses.

Hymn Study: Sing together all the stanzas of "Like a River Glorious," pages 14 and 15 in *Singing the Great Hymns*.

Foreign Language: Work on a series from *Speaking [Spanish] with Miss Mason and Francois*.

Handicrafts: Watch session 3 of the *Handicrafts Made Simple: Hand Sewing* DVD and begin hemming the blanket.

Family Read-Aloud: Continue reading your selection below.
Young Selection: Read together *The Trumpet of the Swan*, chapter 14, "Boston."
Middle Selection: Read together *The Pilgrim's Progress*, beginning where you left off last time through Christian and Faithful's discussion on their journeys ("I thought I should have been killed there, over and over; but at last day broke, and the sun rose, and I went through that which was behind with far more ease and quiet.").
Older Selection: Read together or assign as independent reading *The Hobbit*, the last half of chapter 8, "Flies and Spiders."

Reminder: Get All-of-a-Kind Family *for lesson 24 for those reading the Young Selection books.*

Lesson 15

Materials Needed

- Verse Pack 1
- *Journaling a Year in Nature*, pencils, watercolor paints, field guides
- *Enjoy the Poems of Robert Louis Stevenson*
- *The Trumpet of the Swan* OR *The Pilgrim's Progress* OR *The Hobbit*

Book of Centuries Timeline

Scripture Memory: Work on learning a passage from Verse Pack 1 and review previously memorized verses.

Nature Study: Select and complete a nature study for this season from *Journaling a Year in Nature.*

Poem Repetition: Read aloud the poem "My Shadow" from *Enjoy the Poems of Robert Louis Stevenson*, page 10, and invite students to join in on the parts they know. Encourage students to say beautiful words in a beautiful way from the beginning.

Family Read-Aloud: Continue reading your selection below.
Young Selection: Read together *The Trumpet of the Swan*, chapter 15, "A Night at the Ritz."
Middle Selection: Read together *The Pilgrim's Progress*, beginning where you left off last time through Talkative's departure and Christian and Faithful's entrance into a wilderness ("Thus they went on talking of what they had seen by the way, and so made that way easy which would otherwise, no doubt, have been tedious to them; for now they went through a wilderness.")
Older Selection: Read together or assign as independent reading *The Hobbit*, the first half of chapter 9, "Barrels Out of Bond."

Lesson 16

wk4

Materials Needed

- Verse Pack 1
- *Laying Down the Rails for Children*
- *Picture Study Portfolio: Rembrandt*
- *The Trumpet of the Swan* OR *The Pilgrim's Progress* OR *The Hobbit*

Scripture Memory: Work on learning a passage from Verse Pack 1 and review previously memorized verses.

Habits: Read aloud one lesson from your selected habit in *Laying Down the Rails for Children.*

Picture Study: Ask students what they recall about *The Night Watch.* Do a picture study of *The Return of the Prodigal Son* from Picture Study Portfolio: Rembrandt, then discuss its Leading Thoughts on page 19 of the book.

Family Read-Aloud: Continue reading your selection below.
Young Selection: Read together *The Trumpet of the Swan*, chapter 16, "Philadelphia."
Middle Selection: Read together *The Pilgrim's Progress*, beginning where you left off last time through Christian and Faithful's captivity in Vanity Fair ("but committing themselves to the all-wise disposal of Him that ruleth all things, with much content, they abode in the condition in which they were, until they should be otherwise disposed of.").
Older Selection: Read together or assign as independent reading *The Hobbit*, the last half of chapter 9, "Barrels Out of Bond."

Book of Centuries Timeline

Lesson 17

Materials Needed
- Verse Pack 1
- *Singing the Great Hymns*
- *Enjoy the Poems of Robert Louis Stevenson*
- *Speaking [Spanish] with Miss Mason and Francois*
- *The Trumpet of the Swan* OR *The Pilgrim's Progress* OR *The Hobbit*

Scripture Memory: Work on learning a passage from Verse Pack 1 and review previously memorized verses.

Hymn Study: Sing together all the stanzas of "I Sing the Mighty Power of God," pages 12 and 13 in *Singing the Great Hymns.*

Poetry: Read together "Nest Eggs" from *Enjoy the Poems of Robert Louis Stevenson*, page 11.

Foreign Language: Work on a series from *Speaking [Spanish] with Miss Mason and Francois.*

Family Read-Aloud: Continue reading your selection below.
Young Selection: Read together *The Trumpet of the Swan*, chapter 17, "Serena."
Middle Selection: Read together *The Pilgrim's Progress*, beginning where you left off last time through Christian's eulogy for Faithful ("Sing, Faithful, sing, and let thy name survive; For though they kill'd thee, thou art yet alive!").
Older Selection: Read together or assign as independent reading *The Hobbit*, chapter 10, "A Warm Welcome."

Reminder: *Get* Bambi: A Life in the Woods *for lesson 27 for those reading the Middle Selection books.*

Lesson 18

Materials Needed
- Verse Pack 1
- *Laying Down the Rails for Children*
- *Music Study with the Masters: J. S. Bach*
- Book of Centuries
- *The Trumpet of the Swan* OR *The Pilgrim's Progress* OR *The Hobbit*

Scripture Memory: Work on learning a passage from Verse Pack 1 and review previously memorized verses.

Johann Sebastian Bach, composer (1685–1750)

Habits: Read aloud one lesson from your selected habit in *Laying Down the Rails for Children.*

Book of Centuries Timeline

Music Study: Read together "A Day in the Life of J. S. Bach" on pages 9–15 in the *Music Study with the Masters: J. S. Bach* book and ask for an oral narration. Enter J. S. Bach in your Book of Centuries.

Tip: *Don't forget to listen to Bach's music sometime today or this week.*

Family Read-Aloud: Continue reading your selection below.
Young Selection: Read together *The Trumpet of the Swan*, chapter 18, "Freedom."
Middle Selection: Read together *The Pilgrim's Progress*, beginning where you left off last time through Christian's reply to Mr. Hold-the-world's question ("And if they are mute when dealt with by vessels of clay, what will they do when they shall be rebuked by the flames of a devouring fire?").
Older Selection: Read together or assign as independent reading *The Hobbit*, chapter 11, "On the Doorstep."

Lesson 19

Materials Needed

- Verse Pack 1
- *Singing the Great Hymns*
- *Speaking [Spanish] with Miss Mason and Francois*
- *Handicrafts Made Simple: Hand Sewing* DVD, booklet, and materials
- *The Trumpet of the Swan* OR *The Pilgrim's Progress* OR *The Hobbit*

Scripture Memory: Work on learning a passage from Verse Pack 1 and review previously memorized verses.

Hymn Study: Sing together all the stanzas of "Like a River Glorious," pages 14 and 15 in *Singing the Great Hymns.*

Foreign Language: Work on a series from *Speaking [Spanish] with Miss Mason and Francois.*

Handicrafts: Finish hemming your blanket or make one of the alternate ideas suggested on the DVD, using the running stitch.

Family Read-Aloud: Continue reading your selection below.
Young Selection: Read together *The Trumpet of the Swan*, chapter 19, "A Talk About Money."
Middle Selection: Read together *The Pilgrim's Progress*, beginning where you left off last time through Christian's leading Hopeful out of the way ("Yet they adventured to go back, but it was so dark, and the flood was so high, that in their going back they had like to have been drowned nine or ten times.").
Older Selection: Read together or assign as independent reading *The Hobbit*, the first half of chapter 12, "Inside Information."

Book of Centuries Timeline

Lesson 20

Materials Needed

- Verse Pack 1
- *Journaling a Year in Nature*, pencils, watercolor paints, field guides
- *Enjoy the Poems of Robert Louis Stevenson*
- *The Trumpet of the Swan* OR *The Pilgrim's Progress* OR *The Hobbit*

Scripture Memory: Work on learning a passage from Verse Pack 1 and review previously memorized verses.

Nature Study: Select and complete a nature study for this season from *Journaling a Year in Nature*.

Poem Repetition: Read aloud the poem "My Shadow" from *Enjoy the Poems of Robert Louis Stevenson*, page 10, and invite students to join in on the parts they know. Encourage students to take their time as they speak, not rushing through the words.

Family Read-Aloud: Continue reading your selection below.
Young Selection: Read together *The Trumpet of the Swan*, chapter 20, "Billings."
Middle Selection: Read together *The Pilgrim's Progress*, beginning where you left off last time through the shepherds' cautions as Christian and Hopeful left them ("And third bid them take heed that they sleep not upon the Enchanted Ground. And the fourth bid them God-speed. So I awoke from my dream.").
Older Selection: Read together or assign as independent reading *The Hobbit*, the last half of chapter 12, "Inside Information."

Lesson 21

Materials Needed

- Verse Pack 1
- *Laying Down the Rails for Children*
- *Picture Study Portfolio: Rembrandt*
- *The Trumpet of the Swan* OR *The Pilgrim's Progress* OR *The Hobbit*

Scripture Memory: Work on learning a passage from Verse Pack 1 and review previously memorized verses.

Habits: Read aloud one lesson from your selected habit in *Laying Down the Rails for Children.*

Picture Study: Ask students what they recall about *The Return of the Prodigal Son.* Do a picture study of *Jacob Blessing Joseph's Second Son* from *Picture Study Portfolio: Rembrandt*, then discuss its Leading Thoughts on page 19 of the book.

Family Read-Aloud: Continue reading your selection below.
Young Selection: Read together *The Trumpet of the Swan*, chapter 21, "The Greening Spring."

Middle Selection: Read together *The Pilgrim's Progress*, beginning where you left off last time through Christian and Hopeful and Ignorance's discussion about thieves on the King's highway ("Poor Little-faith! Hast been among the thieves? Wast robb'd? Remember this, whoso believes, And gets more faith, shall then a victor be Over ten thousand, else scarce over three.").
Older Selection: Read together or assign as independent reading *The Hobbit*, the first half of chapter 13, "Not at Home."

Reminder: Get The Fellowship of the Ring *for lesson 31 for those reading the Older Selection books.*

Lesson 22

Materials Needed
- Verse Pack 1
- *Singing the Great Hymns*
- *Enjoy the Poems of Robert Louis Stevenson*
- *Speaking [Spanish] with Miss Mason and Francois*
- *The Trumpet of the Swan* OR *The Pilgrim's Progress* OR *The Hobbit*

Scripture Memory: Work on learning a passage from Verse Pack 1 and review previously memorized verses.

Hymn Study: Sing together all the stanzas of "I Sing the Mighty Power of God," pages 12 and 13 in *Singing the Great Hymns*.

Poetry: Read together "Block City" from *Enjoy the Poems of Robert Louis Stevenson*, page 12.

Foreign Language: Work on a series from *Speaking [Spanish] with Miss Mason and Francois*.

Family Read-Aloud: Continue reading your selection below.
Young Selection: Use today and tomorrow to catch up as needed and finish *The Trumpet of the Swan*.
Middle Selection: Read together *The Pilgrim's Progress*, beginning where you left off last time through Christian and Hopeful's conversation about Hopeful's experience ("It made me love a holy life, and long to do something for the honour and glory of the name of the Lord Jesus; yea, I thought that had I now a thousand gallons of blood in my body, I could spill it all for the sake of the Lord Jesus.")
Older Selection: Read together or assign as independent reading *The Hobbit*, the last half of chapter 13, "Not at Home."

Lesson 23

Materials Needed
- Verse Pack 1

Book of Centuries Timeline

Book of Centuries Timeline

- *Laying Down the Rails for Children*
- *Music Study with the Masters: J. S. Bach*
- *The Trumpet of the Swan* OR *The Pilgrim's Progress* OR *The Hobbit*

Scripture Memory: Work on learning a passage from Verse Pack 1 and review previously memorized verses.

Habits: Read aloud one lesson from your selected habit in *Laying Down the Rails for Children.*

Music Study: Use the Listen and Learn notes on pages 36 and 37 in the *Music Study with the Masters: J. S. Bach* book to help you listen to and discuss *Toccata and Fugue in D Minor.* Older students should also read Part 1 of "The Story of J. S. Bach," beginning on page 17.

Family Read-Aloud: Continue reading your selection below.
Young Selection: Use today to catch up as needed and finish *The Trumpet of the Swan.*
Middle Selection: Read together *The Pilgrim's Progress*, beginning where you left off last time through Christian and Hopeful's discussion on backsliders ("Thus, being launched again into the gulf of misery, unless a miracle of grace prevent it, they everlastingly perish in their own deceivings.").
Older Selection: Read together or assign as independent reading *The Hobbit*, chapter 14, "Fire and Water."

Lesson 24

Materials Needed

- Verse Pack 1
- *Singing the Great Hymns*
- *Speaking [Spanish] with Miss Mason and Francois*
- *Handicrafts Made Simple: Hand Sewing* DVD, booklet, and materials
- *All-of-a-Kind Family* OR *The Pilgrim's Progress* OR *The Hobbit*

Scripture Memory: Work on learning a passage from Verse Pack 1 and review previously memorized verses.

Hymn Study: Sing together all the stanzas of "Like a River Glorious," pages 14 and 15 in *Singing the Great Hymns.*

Foreign Language: Work on a series from *Speaking [Spanish] with Miss Mason and Francois.*

All-of-a-Kind Family *(1910)*

Handicrafts: Watch session 4 of the *Handicrafts Made Simple: Hand Sewing* DVD and sew the bag.

Family Read-Aloud: Continue reading your selection below.
Young Selection: Read together *All-of-a-Kind Family*, chapter 1, "The Library Lady."
Middle Selection: Read together *The Pilgrim's Progress*, beginning where you

left off last time through The Conclusion ("But if thou shalt cast all away as vain, I know not but 'twill make me dream again.").
Older Selection: Read together or assign as independent reading *The Hobbit*, chapter 15, "The Gathering of the Clouds."

Book of Centuries Timeline

Lesson 25

Materials Needed

- Verse Pack 1
- *Journaling a Year in Nature*, pencils, watercolor paints, field guides
- *Enjoy the Poems of Robert Louis Stevenson*
- *All-of-a-Kind Family* OR *The Pilgrim's Progress* OR *The Hobbit*

Scripture Memory: Work on learning a passage from Verse Pack 1 and review previously memorized verses.

Nature Study: Select and complete a nature study for this season from *Journaling a Year in Nature.*

Poem Repetition: Read aloud the poem "My Shadow" from *Enjoy the Poems of Robert Louis Stevenson*, page 10, and invite students to join in on the parts they know.

Family Read-Aloud: Continue reading your selection below.
Young Selection: Read together *All-of-a-Kind Family*, chapter 2, "Dusting Is Fun."
Middle Selection: Use today and tomorrow as needed to finish reading *The Pilgrim's Progress.*
Older Selection: Read together or assign as independent reading *The Hobbit*, chapter 16, "A Thief in the Night."

Lesson 26

wk 6

Materials Needed

- Verse Pack 1
- *Laying Down the Rails for Children*
- *Picture Study Portfolio: Rembrandt*
- *All-of-a-Kind Family* OR *The Pilgrim's Progress* OR *The Hobbit*

Scripture Memory: Work on learning a passage from Verse Pack 1 and review previously memorized verses.

Habits: Read aloud one lesson from your selected habit in *Laying Down the Rails for Children.*

Picture Study: Ask students what they recall about *Jacob Blessing Joseph's Second Son.* Do a picture study of *Titus as a Monk* from *Picture Study Portfolio: Rembrandt*, then discuss its Leading Thoughts on page 20 of the book.

Family Read-Aloud: Continue reading your selection below.

Book of Centuries Timeline

Young Selection: Read together *All-of-a-Kind Family*, chapter 3, "Rainy Day Surprise."
Middle Selection: Use today as needed to finish reading *The Pilgrim's Progress.*
Older Selection: Read together or assign as independent reading *The Hobbit*, the first half of chapter 17, "The Clouds Burst."

Lesson 27

Materials Needed

- Verse Pack 1
- *Singing the Great Hymns*
- *Enjoy the Poems of Robert Louis Stevenson*
- Book of Centuries
- *Speaking [Spanish] with Miss Mason and Francois*
- *All-of-a-Kind Family* OR *Bambi: A Life in the Woods* OR *The Hobbit*

Robert Louis Stevenson, author and poet (1850–1894)

Scripture Memory: Work on learning a passage from Verse Pack 1 and review previously memorized verses.

Hymn Study: Sing together all the stanzas of "To God Be the Glory," pages 16 and 17 in *Singing the Great Hymns.*

Poetry: Show students the picture of Robert Louis Stevenson and ask them what they recall about him. Enter him in your Book of Centuries.

Foreign Language: Work on a series from *Speaking [Spanish] with Miss Mason and Francois.*

Family Read-Aloud: Continue reading your selection below.
Young Selection: Read together *All-of-a-Kind Family*, chapter 4, "Who Cares If It's Bedtime?"
Middle Selection: Read together *Bambi: A Life in the Woods*, chapter 1.
Older Selection: Read together or assign as independent reading *The Hobbit*, the last half of chapter 17, "The Clouds Burst."

Lesson 28

Materials Needed

- Verse Pack 1
- *Laying Down the Rails for Children*
- *Music Study with the Masters: J. S. Bach*
- *All-of-a-Kind Family* OR *Bambi: A Life in the Woods* OR *The Hobbit*

Scripture Memory: Work on learning a passage from Verse Pack 1 and review previously memorized verses.

Habits: Read aloud one lesson from your selected habit in *Laying Down the Rails for Children.*

Music Study: Use the Listen and Learn notes on page 38 in the *Music Study with the Masters: J. S. Bach* book to help you listen to and discuss *Minuet in G Major.* Older students should also read Part 2 of "The Story of J. S. Bach," beginning on page 22.

Family Read-Aloud: Continue reading your selection below.
Young Selection: Read together *All-of-a-Kind Family*, chapter 5, "The Sabbath."
Middle Selection: Read together *Bambi: A Life in the Woods*, chapter 2.
Older Selection: Read together or assign as independent reading *The Hobbit*, chapter 18, "The Return Journey."

Lesson 29

Materials Needed

- Verse Pack 1
- *Singing the Great Hymns*
- *Speaking [Spanish] with Miss Mason and Francois*
- *Handicrafts Made Simple: Hand Sewing* DVD, booklet, and materials
- *All-of-a-Kind Family* OR *Bambi: A Life in the Woods* OR *The Hobbit*

Scripture Memory: Work on learning a passage from Verse Pack 1 and review previously memorized verses.

Hymn Study: Sing together all the stanzas of "I Sing the Mighty Power of God," pages 12 and 13 in *Singing the Great Hymns.*

Foreign Language: Work on a series from *Speaking [Spanish] with Miss Mason and Francois.*

Handicrafts: Watch session 5 of the *Handicrafts Made Simple: Hand Sewing* DVD and sew the button on the bag.

Family Read-Aloud: Continue reading your selection below.
Young Selection: Read together *All-of-a-Kind Family*, chapter 6, "Papa's Birthday."
Middle Selection: Read together *Bambi: A Life in the Woods*, chapter 3.
Older Selection: Read together or assign as independent reading *The Hobbit*, chapter 19, "The Last Stage."

Reminder: *Get* The Complete Tales of Winnie-the-Pooh *for lesson 39 for those reading the Young Selection books.*

Lesson 30

Materials Needed

- Verse Pack 1
- *Journaling a Year in Nature*, pencils, watercolor paints, field guides
- *Enjoy the Poems of Robert Louis Stevenson*

Book of Centuries Timeline

Book of Centuries Timeline

- *All-of-a-Kind Family* OR *Bambi: A Life in the Woods* OR *The Hobbit*

Scripture Memory: Work on learning a passage from Verse Pack 1 and review previously memorized verses.

Nature Study: Select and complete a nature study for this season from *Journaling a Year in Nature.*

Poem Repetition: Read aloud the poem "My Shadow" from *Enjoy the Poems of Robert Louis Stevenson*, page 10, and invite students to join in on the parts they know. Encourage students to enunciate clearly. If a student is leaving off final consonant sounds (for example, a final *t* or *d* or substituting *in'* for *ing*), point out that bad habit and help him practice speaking those words correctly.

Family Read-Aloud: Continue reading your selection below.
Young Selection: Read together *All-of-a-Kind Family*, chapter 7, "Purim Play."
Middle Selection: Read together *Bambi: A Life in the Woods*, chapter 4.
Older Selection: Use today to finish reading *The Hobbit* if needed.

Lesson 31

Materials Needed
- Verse Pack 1
- *Laying Down the Rails for Children*
- *Picture Study Portfolio: Rembrandt*
- *All-of-a-Kind Family* OR *Bambi: A Life in the Woods* OR *The Fellowship of the Ring*

Scripture Memory: Work on learning a passage from Verse Pack 1 and review previously memorized verses.

Habits: Select a new habit to focus on. Read aloud one lesson from your selected habit in *Laying Down the Rails for Children.*

Picture Study: Ask students what they recall about *Titus as a Monk*. Do a picture study of *The Denial of Peter* from *Picture Study Portfolio: Rembrandt*, then discuss its Leading Thoughts on page 21 of the book.

Family Read-Aloud: Continue reading your selection below.
Young Selection: Read together *All-of-a-Kind Family*, chapter 8, "Sarah In Trouble."
Middle Selection: Read together *Bambi: A Life in the Woods*, chapter 5.
Older Selection: Read together or assign as independent reading *The Fellowship of the Ring*, Book I, the first half of chapter 1, "A Long-Expected Party."

Lesson 32

Materials Needed
- Verse Pack 1

Book of Centuries
Timeline

- *Singing the Great Hymns*
- *Enjoy the Poems of Robert Louis Stevenson*
- *Speaking [Spanish] with Miss Mason and Francois*
- *All-of-a-Kind Family* OR *Bambi: A Life in the Woods* OR *The Fellowship of the Ring*

Scripture Memory: Work on learning a passage from Verse Pack 1 and review previously memorized verses.

Hymn Study: Sing together all the stanzas of "To God Be the Glory," pages 16 and 17 in *Singing the Great Hymns.*

Poetry: Read together "The Swing" from *Enjoy the Poems of Robert Louis Stevenson*, page 13.

Foreign Language: Work on a series from *Speaking [Spanish] with Miss Mason and Francois.*

Family Read-Aloud: Continue reading your selection below.
Young Selection: Read together *All-of-a-Kind Family*, chapter 9, "Mama Has Her Hands Full."
Middle Selection: Read together *Bambi: A Life in the Woods*, chapter 6.
Older Selection: Read together or assign as independent reading *The Fellowship of the Ring*, Book I, the last half of chapter 1, "A Long-Expected Party."

Lesson 33

Materials Needed

- Verse Pack 1
- *Laying Down the Rails for Children*
- *Music Study with the Masters: J. S. Bach*
- *All-of-a-Kind Family* OR *Bambi: A Life in the Woods* OR *The Fellowship of the Ring*

Scripture Memory: Work on learning a passage from Verse Pack 1 and review previously memorized verses.

Habits: Read aloud one lesson from your selected habit in *Laying Down the Rails for Children.*

Music Study: Listen to music by J. S. Bach from *Music Study with the Masters: J. S. Bach.* Older students should also read Part 3 of "The Story of J. S. Bach," beginning on page 28, and give a written narration of the composer's life.

Tip: You can listen to your music study composer while eating lunch, running errands, sitting quietly, or getting ready for bed. Find a time that works well for your family during this season of life.

Book of Centuries Timeline

Family Read-Aloud: Continue reading your selection below.
Young Selection: Read together *All-of-a-Kind Family*, chapter 10, "Fourth of July."
Middle Selection: Read together *Bambi: A Life in the Woods*, chapter 7.
Older Selection: Read together or assign as independent reading *The Fellowship of the Ring*, Book I, the first third of chapter 2, "The Shadow of the Past" (about 10 pages or so).

Lesson 34

Materials Needed

- Verse Pack 1
- *Singing the Great Hymns*
- *Speaking [Spanish] with Miss Mason and Francois*
- Hand-sewing materials
- *All-of-a-Kind Family* OR *Bambi: A Life in the Woods* OR *The Fellowship of the Ring*

Scripture Memory: Work on learning a passage from Verse Pack 1 and review previously memorized verses.

Hymn Study: Sing together all the stanzas of "Like a River Glorious," pages 14 and 15 in *Singing the Great Hymns*.

Foreign Language: Work on a series from *Speaking [Spanish] with Miss Mason and Francois*.

Handicrafts: Have the students sew on any buttons that have come off shirts or clothing at your house.

Family Read-Aloud: Continue reading your selection below.
Young Selection: Read together *All-of-a-Kind Family*, chapter 11, "Family Outing."
Middle Selection: Read together *Bambi: A Life in the Woods*, chapter 8.
Older Selection: Read together or assign as independent reading *The Fellowship of the Ring*, Book I, the next third of chapter 2, "The Shadow of the Past" (another 10 pages or so).

Lesson 35

Materials Needed

- Verse Pack 1
- *Journaling a Year in Nature*, pencils, watercolor paints, field guides
- *Enjoy the Poems of Robert Louis Stevenson*
- *All-of-a-Kind Family* OR *Bambi: A Life in the Woods* OR *The Fellowship of the Ring*

Scripture Memory: Work on learning a passage from Verse Pack 1 and review previously memorized verses.

Nature Study: Select and complete a nature study for this season from *Journaling a Year in Nature.*

Poem Repetition: Read aloud the poem "My Shadow" from *Enjoy the Poems of Robert Louis Stevenson*, page 10, and invite students to join in on the parts they know. Encourage students to say beautiful words in a beautiful way.

Family Read-Aloud: Continue reading your selection below.
Young Selection: Read together *All-of-a-Kind Family*, chapter 12, "Succos."
Middle Selection: Read together *Bambi: A Life in the Woods*, chapter 9.
Older Selection: Read together or assign as independent reading *The Fellowship of the Ring*, Book I, the rest of chapter 2, "The Shadow of the Past."

Lesson 36

Materials Needed

- Verse Pack 1
- *Laying Down the Rails for Children*
- *Picture Study Portfolio: Rembrandt*
- *All-of-a-Kind Family* OR *Bambi: A Life in the Woods* OR *The Fellowship of the Ring*

Scripture Memory: Work on learning a passage from Verse Pack 1 and review previously memorized verses.

Habits: Read aloud one lesson from your selected habit in *Laying Down the Rails for Children.*

Picture Study: Ask students what they recall about *The Denial of Peter.* Do a picture study of *Self-Portrait* from *Picture Study Portfolio: Rembrandt*, then discuss its Leading Thoughts on page 21 of the book.

Family Read-Aloud: Continue reading your selection below.
Young Selection: Read together *All-of-a-Kind Family*, chapter 13, "A New Charlie."
Middle Selection: Read together *Bambi: A Life in the Woods*, chapter 10.
Older Selection: Read together or assign as independent reading *The Fellowship of the Ring*, Book I, the first half of chapter 3, "Three Is Company."

Lesson 37

Materials Needed

- Verse Pack 1
- *Singing the Great Hymns*
- *Enjoy the Poems of Robert Louis Stevenson*
- *Speaking [Spanish] with Miss Mason and Francois*
- *All-of-a-Kind Family* OR *Bambi: A Life in the Woods* OR *The Fellowship of the Ring*

Book of Centuries Timeline

Book of Centuries Timeline

Scripture Memory: Work on learning a passage from Verse Pack 1 and review previously memorized verses.

Hymn Study: Sing together all the stanzas of "To God Be the Glory," pages 16 and 17 in *Singing the Great Hymns.*

Poetry: Read together "My Bed is a Boat" from *Enjoy the Poems of Robert Louis Stevenson*, page 14.

Foreign Language: Work on a series from *Speaking [Spanish] with Miss Mason and Francois.*

Family Read-Aloud: Continue reading your selection below.
Young Selection: Use today and tomorrow to catch up as needed and finish *All-of-a-Kind Family.*
Middle Selection: Read together *Bambi: A Life in the Woods*, chapter 11.
Older Selection: Read together or assign as independent reading *The Fellowship of the Ring*, Book I, the last half of chapter 3, "Three Is Company."

Lesson 38

Materials Needed
- Verse Pack 1
- *Laying Down the Rails for Children*
- *Music Study with the Masters: J. S. Bach*
- *All-of-a-Kind Family* OR *Bambi: A Life in the Woods* OR *The Fellowship of the Ring*

Scripture Memory: Work on learning a passage from Verse Pack 1 and review previously memorized verses.

Habits: Read aloud one lesson from your selected habit in *Laying Down the Rails for Children.*

Music Study: Use the Listen and Learn notes on page 39 in the *Music Study with the Masters: J. S. Bach* book to help you listen to and discuss *Erbarme dich, mein Gott* and *O Haupt voll Blut und Wunden* from *St. Matthew Passion.*

Family Read-Aloud: Continue reading your selection below.
Young Selection: Use today to catch up as needed and finish *All-of-a-Kind Family.*
Middle Selection: Read together *Bambi: A Life in the Woods*, chapter 12.
Older Selection: Read together or assign as independent reading *The Fellowship of the Ring*, Book I, chapter 4, "A Short Cut to Mushrooms."

Lesson 39

Materials Needed
- Verse Pack 1

Book of Centuries Timeline

- *Singing the Great Hymns*
- *Speaking [Spanish] with Miss Mason and Francois*
- *Handicrafts Made Simple: Hand Sewing* DVD, booklet, and materials
- *The Complete Tales of Winnie-the-Pooh* OR *Bambi: A Life in the Woods* OR *The Fellowship of the Ring*

Scripture Memory: Work on learning a passage from Verse Pack 1 and review previously memorized verses.

Hymn Study: Sing together all the stanzas of "I Sing the Mighty Power of God," pages 12 and 13 in *Singing the Great Hymns.*

Foreign Language: Work on a series from *Speaking [Spanish] with Miss Mason and Francois.*

Handicrafts: Watch session 6 of the *Handicrafts Made Simple: Hand Sewing* DVD and sew the felt pillow.

Family Read-Aloud: Continue reading your selection below.
Young Selection: Read together *The Complete Tales of Winnie-the-Pooh*, chapter 1, "In Which We Are Introduced to Winnie-the-Pooh and Some Bees, and the Stories Begin."
Middle Selection: Read together *Bambi: A Life in the Woods*, chapter 13.
Older Selection: Read together or assign as independent reading *The Fellowship of the Ring*, Book I, chapter 5, "A Conspiracy Unmasked."

Lesson 40

Materials Needed

- Verse Pack 1
- *Journaling a Year in Nature*, pencils, watercolor paints, field guides
- *Enjoy the Poems of Robert Louis Stevenson*
- *The Complete Tales of Winnie-the-Pooh* OR *Bambi: A Life in the Woods* OR *The Fellowship of the Ring*

Scripture Memory: Work on learning a passage from Verse Pack 1 and review previously memorized verses.

Nature Study: Select and complete a nature study for this season from *Journaling a Year in Nature.*

Poem Repetition: Read aloud the poem "My Shadow" from *Enjoy the Poems of Robert Louis Stevenson*, page 10, and invite students to join in on the parts they know. Encourage students to consider the ideas contained in the poem and think about how they can best communicate those ideas as they speak.

Family Read-Aloud: Continue reading your selection below.
Young Selection: Read together *The Complete Tales of Winnie-the-Pooh*, chapter 2, "In Which Pooh Goes Visiting and Gets Into a Tight Place."
Middle Selection: Read together *Bambi: A Life in the Woods*, chapter 14.

Book of Centuries Timeline

Older Selection: Read together or assign as independent reading *The Fellowship of the Ring*, Book I, the first half of chapter 6, "The Old Forest."

Lesson 41

Materials Needed

- Verse Pack 1
- *Laying Down the Rails for Children*
- *Picture Study Portfolio: Rembrandt*
- *The Complete Tales of Winnie-the-Pooh* OR *Bambi: A Life in the Woods* OR *The Fellowship of the Ring*

Scripture Memory: Work on learning a passage from Verse Pack 1 and review previously memorized verses.

Habits: Read aloud one lesson from your selected habit in *Laying Down the Rails for Children.*

Picture Study: Ask students what they recall about Rembrandt's *Self-Portrait* studied last time. Do a picture study of *Christ Shows His Wounds to Doubting Thomas* from *Picture Study Portfolio: Rembrandt*, then discuss its Leading Thoughts on page 22 of the book.

Family Read-Aloud: Continue reading your selection below.
Young Selection: Read together *The Complete Tales of Winnie-the-Pooh*, chapter 3, "In Which Pooh and Piglet Go Hunting and Nearly Catch a Woozle."
Middle Selection: Read together *Bambi: A Life in the Woods*, chapter 15.
Older Selection: Read together or assign as independent reading *The Fellowship of the Ring*, Book I, the last half of chapter 6, "The Old Forest."

Lesson 42

Materials Needed

- Verse Pack 1
- *Singing the Great Hymns*
- *Enjoy the Poems of Robert Louis Stevenson*
- *Speaking [Spanish] with Miss Mason and Francois*
- *The Complete Tales of Winnie-the-Pooh* OR *Bambi: A Life in the Woods* OR *The Fellowship of the Ring*

Scripture Memory: Work on learning a passage from Verse Pack 1 and review previously memorized verses.

Hymn Study: Sing together all the stanzas of "To God Be the Glory," pages 16 and 17 in *Singing the Great Hymns.*

Poetry: Invite each student to select one of the poems (or a portion of a poem) that has been read from *Enjoy the Poems of Robert Louis Stevenson* and illustrate it. Pages are provided in the back of the poetry book for illustrations.

You may also create the illustration on a different sheet of paper and tuck it inside the poetry book.

Tip: Make sure each student signs and dates his or her drawing and notes which poem it illustrates.

Foreign Language: Work on a series from *Speaking [Spanish] with Miss Mason and Francois.*

Family Read-Aloud: Continue reading your selection below.
Young Selection: Read together *The Complete Tales of Winnie-the-Pooh,* chapter 4, "In Which Eeyore Loses a Tail and Pooh Finds One."
Middle Selection: Read together *Bambi: A Life in the Woods*, chapter 16.
Older Selection: Read together or assign as independent reading *The Fellowship of the Ring*, Book I, chapter 7, "In the House of Tom Bombadil."

Book of Centuries Timeline

Lesson 43

Materials Needed

- Verse Pack 1
- *Laying Down the Rails for Children*
- *Music Study with the Masters: J. S. Bach*
- *The Complete Tales of Winnie-the-Pooh* OR *Bambi: A Life in the Woods* OR *The Fellowship of the Ring*

Scripture Memory: Work on learning a passage from Verse Pack 1 and review previously memorized verses.

Habits: Read aloud one lesson from your selected habit in *Laying Down the Rails for Children.*

Music Study: Use the Listen and Learn notes on page 40 in the *Music Study with the Masters: J. S. Bach* book to help you listen to and discuss *Prelude and Fugue No. 1 in C Major.*

Family Read-Aloud: Continue reading your selection below.
Young Selection: Read together *The Complete Tales of Winnie-the-Pooh,* chapter 5, "In Which Piglet Meets a Heffalump."
Middle Selection: Read together *Bambi: A Life in the Woods,* chapter 17.
Older Selection: Read together or assign as independent reading *The Fellowship of the Ring*, Book I, the first half of chapter 8, "Fog on the Barrow-Downs."

Lesson 44

Materials Needed

- Verse Pack 1
- *Singing the Great Hymns*

Book of Centuries Timeline

- *Speaking [Spanish] with Miss Mason and Francois*
- *Handicrafts Made Simple: Hand Sewing DVD, booklet, and materials*
- *The Complete Tales of Winnie-the-Pooh* OR *Bambi: A Life in the Woods* OR *The Fellowship of the Ring*

Scripture Memory: Work on learning a passage from Verse Pack 1 and review previously memorized verses.

Hymn Study: Sing together all the stanzas of "Like a River Glorious," pages 14 and 15 in *Singing the Great Hymns.*

Foreign Language: Work on a series from *Speaking [Spanish] with Miss Mason and Francois.*

Handicrafts: Watch session 7 of the *Handicrafts Made Simple: Hand Sewing* DVD and sew the drawstring bag.

Family Read-Aloud: Continue reading your selection below.
Young Selection: Read together *The Complete Tales of Winnie-the-Pooh,* chapter 6, "In Which Eeyore Has a Birthday and Gets Two Presents."
Middle Selection: Read together *Bambi: A Life in the Woods*, chapter 18.
Older Selection: Read together or assign as independent reading *The Fellowship of the Ring*, Book I, the last half of chapter 8, "Fog on the Barrow-Downs."

Reminder: *Get* The Story of the Treasure Seekers *for lesson 54 for those reading the Middle Selection books.*

Lesson 45

Materials Needed

- Verse Pack 1
- *Journaling a Year in Nature*, pencils, watercolor paints, field guides
- *Enjoy the Poems of Robert Louis Stevenson*
- *The Complete Tales of Winnie-the-Pooh* OR *Bambi: A Life in the Woods* OR *The Fellowship of the Ring*

Scripture Memory: Work on learning a passage from Verse Pack 1 and review previously memorized verses.

Nature Study: Select and complete a nature study for this season from *Journaling a Year in Nature.*

Poem Repetition: Read aloud the poem "My Shadow" from *Enjoy the Poems of Robert Louis Stevenson*, page 10, and invite students to join in on the parts they know. Be careful you are not dictating exactly what each student's recitation should sound like. Allow for individual freedom within the boundaries of good communication. Let each child form his own relation with the poet and poem.

Family Read-Aloud: Continue reading your selection below.

Young Selection: Read together *The Complete Tales of Winnie-the-Pooh,* chapter 7, "In Which Kanga and Baby Roo Come to the Forest, and Piglet Has a Bath."
Middle Selection: Read together *Bambi: A Life in the Woods*, chapter 19.
Older Selection: Read together or assign as independent reading *The Fellowship of the Ring*, Book I, the first half of chapter 9, "At the Sign of the Prancing Pony."

Book of Centuries Timeline

Lesson 46

Materials Needed

- Verse Pack 1
- *Laying Down the Rails for Children*
- *Picture Study Portfolio: Rembrandt*
- *The Complete Tales of Winnie-the-Pooh* OR *Bambi: A Life in the Woods* OR *The Fellowship of the Ring*

Scripture Memory: Work on learning a passage from Verse Pack 1 and review previously memorized verses.

Habits: Read aloud one lesson from your selected habit in *Laying Down the Rails for Children.*

Picture Study: Ask students what they recall about *Christ Shows His Wounds to Doubting Thomas*. Do a picture study of *Jacob Wrestling with the Angel* from *Picture Study Portfolio: Rembrandt*, then discuss its Leading Thoughts on page 22 of the book.

Family Read-Aloud: Continue reading your selection below.
Young Selection: Read together *The Complete Tales of Winnie-the-Pooh,* chapter 8, "In Which Christopher Robin Leads an Expotition to the North Pole."
Middle Selection: Read together *Bambi: A Life in the Woods*, chapter 20.
Older Selection: Read together or assign as independent reading *The Fellowship of the Ring*, Book I, the last half of chapter 9, "At the Sign of the Prancing Pony."

Lesson 47

Materials Needed

- Verse Pack 1
- *Singing the Great Hymns*
- *Enjoy the Poems of Robert Louis Stevenson*
- *Speaking [Spanish] with Miss Mason and Francois*
- *The Complete Tales of Winnie-the-Pooh* OR *Bambi: A Life in the Woods* OR *The Fellowship of the Ring*

Scripture Memory: Work on learning a passage from Verse Pack 1 and review previously memorized verses.

Hymn Study: Sing together all the stanzas of "To God Be the Glory," pages 16 and 17 in *Singing the Great Hymns*.

Book of Centuries
Timeline

Poetry: Read together "From a Railway Carriage" from *Enjoy the Poems of Robert Louis Stevenson*, page 15.

Foreign Language: Work on a series from *Speaking [Spanish] with Miss Mason and Francois.*

Family Read-Aloud: Continue reading your selection below.
Young Selection: Read together *The Complete Tales of Winnie-the-Pooh,* chapter 9, "In Which Piglet Is Entirely Surrounded by Water."
Middle Selection: Read together *Bambi: A Life in the Woods*, chapter 21.
Older Selection: Read together or assign as independent reading *The Fellowship of the Ring*, Book I, chapter 10, "Strider."

Lesson 48

Materials Needed

- Verse Pack 1
- *Laying Down the Rails for Children*
- *Music Study with the Masters: J. S. Bach*
- *The Complete Tales of Winnie-the-Pooh* OR *Bambi: A Life in the Woods* OR *The Fellowship of the Ring*

Scripture Memory: Work on learning a passage from Verse Pack 1 and review previously memorized verses.

Habits: Read aloud one lesson from your selected habit in *Laying Down the Rails for Children.*

Music Study: Use the Listen and Learn notes on page 41 in the *Music Study with the Masters: J. S. Bach* book to help you listen to and discuss the *Aria* from *Goldberg Variations.*

Family Read-Aloud: Continue reading your selection below.
Young Selection: Read together *The Complete Tales of Winnie-the-Pooh,* chapter 10, "In Which Christopher Robin Gives Pooh a Party, and We Say Good-bye."
Middle Selection: Read together *Bambi: A Life in the Woods*, chapter 22.
Older Selection: Read together or assign as independent reading *The Fellowship of the Ring*, Book I, the first half of chapter 11, "A Knife in the Dark."

Lesson 49

Materials Needed

- Verse Pack 1
- *Singing the Great Hymns*
- *Speaking [Spanish] with Miss Mason and Francois*
- *Handicrafts Made Simple: Hand Sewing* DVD, booklet, and materials
- *The Complete Tales of Winnie the Pooh* OR *Bambi: A Life in the Woods* OR *The Fellowship of the Ring*

Scripture Memory: Work on learning a passage from Verse Pack 1 and review previously memorized verses.

Hymn Study: Sing together all the stanzas of "I Sing the Mighty Power of God," pages 12 and 13 in *Singing the Great Hymns.*

Foreign Language: Work on a series from *Speaking [Spanish] with Miss Mason and Francois.*

Handicrafts: Watch session 8 of the *Handicrafts Made Simple: Hand Sewing* DVD and begin sewing the four-square blanket.

Family Read-Aloud: Continue reading your selection below.
Young Selection: Read together *The Complete Tales of Winnie-the-Pooh: The House at Pooh Corner,* chapter 1, "In Which a House Is Built at Pooh Corner for Eeyore."
Middle Selection: Read together *Bambi: A Life in the Woods*, chapter 23.
Older Selection: Read together or assign as independent reading *The Fellowship of the Ring*, Book I, the last half of chapter 11, "A Knife in the Dark."

Book of Centuries Timeline

Lesson 50

Materials Needed

- Verse Pack 1
- Journaling a Year in Nature, pencils, watercolor paints, field guides
- Enjoy the Poems of Robert Louis Stevenson
- *The Complete Tales of Winnie-the-Pooh* OR *Bambi: A Life in the Woods* OR *The Fellowship of the Ring*

Scripture Memory: Work on learning a passage from Verse Pack 1 and review previously memorized verses.

Nature Study: Select and complete a nature study for this season from *Journaling a Year in Nature.*

Poem Repetition: Ask the children to read/recite aloud the poem "My Shadow" from *Enjoy the Poems of Robert Louis Stevenson*, page 10. Help them identify any portions that they don't yet know thoroughly or could use more polish in saying aloud. Explain that they will each be asked to recite the poem over the next two weeks.

Family Read-Aloud: Continue reading your selection below.
Young Selection: Read together *The Complete Tales of Winnie-the-Pooh: The House at Pooh Corner*, chapter 2, "In Which Tigger Comes to the Forest and Has Breakfast."
Middle Selection: Read together *Bambi: A Life in the Woods*, chapter 24.
Older Selection: Read together or assign as independent reading *The Fellowship of the Ring*, Book I, the first half of chapter 12, "Flight to the Ford."

Book of Centuries
Timeline

Reminder: Make sure you have the resources you will need for Term 2. See page 53 for details.

Lesson 51

Materials Needed

- Verse Pack 1
- *Laying Down the Rails for Children*
- *Picture Study Portfolio: Rembrandt*
- *The Complete Tales of Winnie-the-Pooh* OR *Bambi: A Life in the Woods* OR *The Fellowship of the Ring*

Scripture Memory: Work on learning a passage from Verse Pack 1 and review previously memorized verses.

Habits: Read aloud one lesson from your selected habit in *Laying Down the Rails for Children.*

Picture Study: Ask students what they recall about *Jacob Wrestling with the Angel.* Use this week to catch up on any Rembrandt picture studies from *Picture Study Portfolio: Rembrandt* or to read a selection from the Recommended Reading list in the book.

Family Read-Aloud: Continue reading your selection below.
Young Selection: Read together *The Complete Tales of Winnie-the-Pooh: The House at Pooh Corner,* chapter 3, "In Which A Search Is Organdized, and Piglet Nearly Meets the Heffalump Again."
Middle Selection: Read together *Bambi: A Life in the Woods,* chapter 25.
Older Selection: Read together or assign as independent reading *The Fellowship of the Ring,* Book I, the last half of chapter 12, "Flight to the Ford."

Lesson 52

Materials Needed

- Verse Pack 1
- *Singing the Great Hymns*
- *Enjoy the Poems of Robert Louis Stevenson*
- *Speaking [Spanish] with Miss Mason and Francois*
- *The Complete Tales of Winnie-the-Pooh* OR *Bambi: A Life in the Woods* OR *The Fellowship of the Ring*

Scripture Memory: Work on learning a passage from Verse Pack 1 and review previously memorized verses.

Hymn Study: Sing together all the stanzas of "To God Be the Glory," pages 16 and 17 in *Singing the Great Hymns.*

Poetry: Read together "A Good Boy" from *Enjoy the Poems of Robert Louis Stevenson,* page 16.

Foreign Language: Work on a series from *Speaking [Spanish] with Miss Mason and Francois.*

Family Read-Aloud: Continue reading your selection below.
Young Selection: Read together *The Complete Tales of Winnie-the-Pooh: The House at Pooh Corner,* chapter 4, "In Which It Is Shown That Tiggers Don't Climb Trees."
Middle Selection: Use today and tomorrow as needed to finish reading *Bambi: A Life in the Woods.*
Older Selection: Use today to catch up on any assigned chapters in *The Fellowship of the Ring,* Book I, if needed.

Lesson 53

Materials Needed

- Verse Pack 1
- *Laying Down the Rails for Children*
- *Music Study with the Masters: J. S. Bach*
- *The Complete Tales of Winnie-the-Pooh* OR *Bambi: A Life in the Woods* OR *The Fellowship of the Ring*

Scripture Memory: Work on learning a passage from Verse Pack 1 and review previously memorized verses.

Habits: Read aloud one lesson from your selected habit in *Laying Down the Rails for Children.*

Music Study: Listen to students' favorite pieces by J. S. Bach from *Music Study with the Masters: J. S. Bach* and ask each person to tell why that piece is his or her favorite.

Family Read-Aloud: Continue reading your selection below.
Young Selection: Read together *The Complete Tales of Winnie-the-Pooh: The House at Pooh Corner,* chapter 5, "In Which Rabbit Has a Busy Day, and We Learn What Christopher Robin Does in the Mornings."
Middle Selection: Use today as needed to finish reading *Bambi: A Life in the Woods.*
Older Selection: Read together or assign as independent reading *The Fellowship of the Ring,* Book II, the first half of chapter 1, "Many Meetings."

Lesson 54

Materials Needed

- Verse Pack 1
- *Singing the Great Hymns*
- *Speaking [Spanish] with Miss Mason and Francois*
- Hand-sewing materials
- *The Complete Tales of Winnie-the-Pooh* OR *The Story of the Treasure*

Book of Centuries Timeline

Book of Centuries Timeline

Seekers OR *The Fellowship of the Ring*

Scripture Memory: Work on learning a passage from Verse Pack 1 and review previously memorized verses.

Hymn Study: Sing together all the stanzas of "Like a River Glorious," pages 14 and 15 in *Singing the Great Hymns.*

Foreign Language: Work on a series from *Speaking [Spanish] with Miss Mason and Francois.*

Handicrafts: Finish sewing the four-square blanket or select another hand sewing project to do.

Family Read-Aloud: Continue reading your selection below.
Young Selection: Read together *The Complete Tales of Winnie-the-Pooh: The House at Pooh Corner,* chapter 6, "In Which Pooh Invents a New Game and Eeyore Joins In."
Middle Selection: Read together *The Story of the Treasure Seekers,* chapter 1, "The Council of Ways and Means."
Older Selection: Read together or assign as independent reading *The Fellowship of the Ring,* Book II, the last half of chapter 1, "Many Meetings."

Lesson 55

Materials Needed

- Verse Pack 1
- *Journaling a Year in Nature,* pencils, watercolor paints, field guides
- *Enjoy the Poems of Robert Louis Stevenson*
- *The Complete Tales of Winnie-the-Pooh* OR *The Story of the Treasure Seekers* OR *The Fellowship of the Ring*

Scripture Memory: Work on learning a passage from Verse Pack 1 and review previously memorized verses.

Nature Study: Select and complete a nature study for this season from *Journaling a Year in Nature.*

Poem Repetition: Ask students to recite aloud the poem "My Shadow" from *Enjoy the Poems of Robert Louis Stevenson,* page 10. Allow any students who are ready to recite the poem alone today. Encourage them to stand before the others and communicate the poem well. Help any children who need final coaching before their individual recitations next week.

Family Read-Aloud: Continue reading your selection below.
Young Selection: Read together *The Complete Tales of Winnie-the-Pooh: The House at Pooh Corner,* chapter 7, "In Which Tigger Is Unbounced."
Middle Selection: Read together *The Story of the Treasure Seekers,* chapter 2, "Digging for Treasure."
Older Selection: Read together or assign as independent reading *The Fellowship*

of the Ring, Book II, the first third of chapter 2, "The Council of Elrond" (about 10 pages or so).

Book of Centuries Timeline

Lesson 56

Materials Needed

- Verse Pack 1
- *Laying Down the Rails for Children*
- *Picture Study Portfolio: Rembrandt*
- *The Complete Tales of Winnie-the-Pooh* OR *The Story of the Treasure Seekers* OR *The Fellowship of the Ring*

Scripture Memory: Work on learning a passage from Verse Pack 1 and review previously memorized verses.

Habits: Read aloud one lesson from your selected habit in *Laying Down the Rails for Children.*

Picture Study: Ask each student to tell about his or her favorite Rembrandt picture. The student may describe his favorite orally, sketch the elements of it, or write a description.

Family Read-Aloud: Continue reading your selection below.
Young Selection: Read together *The Complete Tales of Winnie-the-Pooh: The House at Pooh Corner*, chapter 8, "In Which Piglet Does a Very Grand Thing."
Middle Selection: Read together *The Story of the Treasure Seekers*, chapter 3, "Being Detectives."
Older Selection: Read together or assign as independent reading *The Fellowship of the Ring*, Book II, the next third of chapter 2, "The Council of Elrond" (about 10 pages or so).

Lesson 57

Materials Needed

- Verse Pack 1
- Singing the Great Hymns
- *Enjoy the Poems of Robert Louis Stevenson*
- *Speaking [Spanish] with Miss Mason and Francois*
- *The Complete Tales of Winnie-the-Pooh* OR *The Story of the Treasure Seekers* OR *The Fellowship of the Ring*

Scripture Memory: Work on learning a passage from Verse Pack 1 and review previously memorized verses.

Hymn Study: Sing together a favorite hymn studied so far. If desired, ask a student to sing or quote his favorite stanza.

Poetry: Ask students to tell what they know about Robert Louis Stevenson and his poetry.

Book of Centuries Timeline

Foreign Language: Work on a series from *Speaking [Spanish] with Miss Mason and Francois.*

Family Read-Aloud: Continue reading your selection below.
Young Selection: Read together *The Complete Tales of Winnie-the-Pooh: The House at Pooh Corner*, chapter 9, "In Which Eeyore Finds the Wolery and Owl Moves Into It."
Middle Selection: Read together *The Story of the Treasure Seekers*, chapter 4, "Good Hunting."
Older Selection: Read together or assign as independent reading *The Fellowship of the Ring*, Book II, the rest of chapter 2, "The Council of Elrond."

Lesson 58

Materials Needed

- Verse Pack 1
- *Laying Down the Rails for Children*
- *Music Study with the Masters: J. S. Bach*
- *The Complete Tales of Winnie-the-Pooh* OR *The Story of the Treasure Seekers* OR *The Fellowship of the Ring*

Scripture Memory: Work on learning a passage from Verse Pack 1 and review previously memorized verses.

Habits: Read aloud one lesson from your selected habit in *Laying Down the Rails for Children.*

Music Study: Ask students to tell or write about any three of the compositions of J. S. Bach that they have listened to.

Family Read-Aloud: Continue reading your selection below.
Young Selection: Read together *The Complete Tales of Winnie-the-Pooh: The House at Pooh Corner*, chapter 10, "In Which Christopher Robin and Pooh Come to an Enchanted Place, and We Leave Them There."
Middle Selection: Read together *The Story of the Treasure Seekers*, chapter 5, "The Poet and the Editor."
Older Selection: Read together or assign as independent reading *The Fellowship of the Ring*, Book II, the first half of chapter 3, "The Ring Goes South."

Lesson 59

Materials Needed

- Verse Pack 1
- *Singing the Great Hymns*
- *Speaking [Spanish] with Miss Mason and Francois*
- Hand-sewing materials, if needed
- *The Complete Tales of Winnie-the-Pooh* OR *The Story of the Treasure Seekers* OR *The Fellowship of the Ring*

Scripture Memory: Work on learning a passage from Verse Pack 1 and review previously memorized verses.

Hymn Study: Sing together a favorite hymn studied so far. If desired, ask a student to sing or quote his favorite stanza.

Foreign Language: Work on a series from *Speaking [Spanish] with Miss Mason and Francois.*

Handicrafts: Use this week to catch up on any hand sewing projects.

Family Read-Aloud: Continue reading your selection below.
Young Selection: Use today and tomorrow as needed to catch up and finish *The Complete Tales of Winnie-the-Pooh.*
Middle Selection: Read together *The Story of the Treasure Seekers*, chapter 6, "Noel's Princess."
Older Selection: Read together or assign as independent reading *The Fellowship of the Ring*, Book II, the last half of chapter 3, "The Ring Goes South."

Lesson 60

Materials Needed

- Verse Pack 1
- *Journaling a Year in Nature*, pencils, watercolor paints, field guides
- *Enjoy the Poems of Robert Louis Stevenson*
- *The Complete Tales of Winnie-the-Pooh* OR *The Story of the Treasure Seekers* OR *The Fellowship of the Ring*

Scripture Memory: Work on learning a passage from Verse Pack 1 and review previously memorized verses.

Nature Study: Select and complete a nature study for this season from *Journaling a Year in Nature.*

Poem Repetition: Ask each student who has not already done so to recite aloud the poem "My Shadow" from *Enjoy the Poems of Robert Louis Stevenson*, page 10.

Family Read-Aloud: Continue reading your selection below.
Young Selection: Use today to finish *The Complete Tales of Winnie-the-Pooh* if needed.
Middle Selection: Read together *The Story of the Treasure Seekers*, chapter 7, "Being Bandits."
Older Selection: Read together or assign as independent reading *The Fellowship of the Ring*, Book II, the first third of chapter 4, "A Journey in the Dark" (about 10 pages or so).

Book of Centuries Timeline

Term 2

(12 weeks; 5 lessons/week)

Term 2 Resource List

- Scripture Memory Verse Pack 1
- Book of Centuries (one per family and older student)
- *Creating a Masterpiece*: Pastels video(s) and materials
- *Picture Study Portfolio: Constable*
- *Enjoy the Poems of Robert Louis Stevenson*
- *Music Study with the Masters: Beethoven*
- *Journaling a Year in Nature* (one per person), pencils, watercolor paints, field guides
- *Singing the Great Hymns*
- *Speaking [Spanish] with Miss Mason and Francois* (or your preferred language)
- *Laying Down the Rails for Children*

Plus Family Read-Aloud Books (Select one group.)

Young Group

- *Five Little Peppers and How They Grew*
- *The Wonderful Wizard of Oz*

Middle Group

- *The Story of the Treasure Seekers*
- *The Swiss Family Robinson*

Older Group

- *The Fellowship of the Ring*
- *The Two Towers*
- *The Return of the King*

Suggested Weekly Schedule

Day 1 *(approx. 1+ hour)*	Day 2 *(approx. 1 hour)*	Day 3 *(approx. 1 hour)*	Day 4 *(approx. 1 hour)*	Day 5 *(approx. 1 hour)*
• Scripture Memory (10 min.) • Foreign Language (15 min.) • Nature Study (15+ min.) • Family Read-Aloud (20 min.)	• Scripture Memory (10 min.) • Hymn Study (5 min.) • Art (20 min.) • Family Read-Aloud (20 min.)	• Scripture Memory (10 min.) • Habits (10 min.) • Picture Study (10 min.) • Repetition: Poem (5 min.) • Family Read-Aloud (20 min.)	• Scripture Memory (10 min.) • Hymn Study (5 min.) • Foreign Language (15 min.) • Poetry (5 min.) • Family Read-Aloud (20 min.)	• Scripture Memory (10 min.) • Habits (10 min.) • Music Study (10 min.) • Family Read-Aloud (20 min.)

Lesson 61

Book of Centuries Timeline

Materials Needed
- Verse Pack 1
- *Speaking [Spanish] with Miss Mason and Francois*
- *Journaling a Year in Nature*, pencils, watercolor paints, field guides
- *Five Little Peppers and How They Grew* OR *The Story of the Treasure Seekers* OR *The Fellowship of the Ring*

Scripture Memory: Work on learning a passage from Verse Pack 1 and review previously memorized verses.

Foreign Language: Work on a series from *Speaking [Spanish] with Miss Mason and Francois.*

Nature Study: Select and complete a nature study for this season from *Journaling a Year in Nature.*

Family Read-Aloud: Continue reading your selection below.
Young Selection: Read together *Five Little Peppers and How They Grew*, chapter 1, "A Home View."
Middle Selection: Read together *The Story of the Treasure Seekers*, chapter 8, "Being Editors."
Older Selection: Read together or assign as independent reading *The Fellowship of the Ring*, Book II, the next third of chapter 4, "A Journey in the Dark" (about 10 pages or so).

Five Little Peppers *(1881)*

Tip: Feel free to do the different assignments at various times throughout the day. For example, you may want to do Scripture Memory at breakfast or save Poetry for a special treat at Tea Time or do your Family Read-Aloud at bedtime. Make your schedule your servant, not your master.

Lesson 62

Materials Needed
- Verse Pack 1
- *Singing the Great Hymns*
- *Creating a Masterpiece:* Pastels video and materials
- *Five Little Peppers and How They Grew* OR *The Story of the Treasure Seekers* OR *The Fellowship of the Ring*

Scripture Memory: Work on learning a passage from Verse Pack 1 and review previously memorized verses.

Hymn Study: Sing together all desired stanzas of "O Come, All Ye Faithful," pages 24 and 25 in *Singing the Great Hymns.*

Book of Centuries Timeline

Tip: Feel free to adjust the dates you learn this hymn or substitute a different hymn as desired.

Art: Work on a pastels project.

Family Read-Aloud: Continue reading your selection below.
Young Selection: Read together *Five Little Peppers and How They Grew,* chapter 2, "Making Happiness for Mamsie."
Middle Selection: Read together *The Story of the Treasure Seekers*, chapter 9, "The G. B."
Older Selection: Read together or assign as independent reading *The Fellowship of the Ring*, Book II, the rest of chapter 4, "A Journey in the Dark."

Reminder: *Get* The Swiss Family Robinson *for lesson 72 for those reading the Middle Selection books.*

Lesson 63

Materials Needed
- Verse Pack 1
- *Laying Down the Rails for Children*
- *Picture Study Portfolio: Constable*
- *Enjoy the Poems of Robert Louis Stevenson*
- *Five Little Peppers and How They Grew* OR *The Story of the Treasure Seekers* OR *The Fellowship of the Ring*

Scripture Memory: Work on learning a passage from Verse Pack 1 and review previously memorized verses.

Habits: Select a new habit to focus on. Read aloud one lesson from your selected habit in *Laying Down the Rails for Children.*

Picture Study: Read together the first half of "The Story of Constable" from *Picture Study Portfolio: Constable*, pages 11 and 12, and ask for an oral narration. Be sure to show the students the portrait of Constable on the cover of the book.

Poem Repetition: Ask each student to select a poem that has been read from *Enjoy the Poems of Robert Louis Stevenson* to learn over the next few weeks.

Tip: *If it would be easier, you may assign one poem for all the children to learn instead.*

Family Read-Aloud: Continue reading your selection below.

Young Selection: Read together *Five Little Peppers and How They Grew*, chapter 3, "Mamsie's Birthday."
Middle Selection: Read together *The Story of the Treasure Seekers*, chapter 10, "Lord Tottenham."
Older Selection: Read together or assign as independent reading *The Fellowship of the Ring*, Book II, chapter 5, "The Bridge of Khazad-dum."

Reminder: Get The Two Towers *for lesson 73 for those reading the Older Selection books.*

Lesson 64

Materials Needed

- Verse Pack 1
- *Singing the Great Hymns*
- *Speaking [Spanish] with Miss Mason and Francois*
- *Enjoy the Poems of Robert Louis Stevenson*
- *Five Little Peppers and How They Grew* OR *The Story of the Treasure Seekers* OR *The Fellowship of the Ring*

Scripture Memory: Work on learning a passage from Verse Pack 1 and review previously memorized verses.

Hymn Study: Sing together all the stanzas of "To God Be the Glory," pages 16 and 17 in *Singing the Great Hymns*.

Foreign Language: Work on a series from *Speaking [Spanish] with Miss Mason and Francois*.

Poetry: Read together "Foreign Lands" from *Enjoy the Poems of Robert Louis Stevenson*, page 17.

Family Read-Aloud: Continue reading your selection below.
Young Selection: Read together *Five Little Peppers and How They Grew*, chapter 4, "Trouble for the Little Brown House."
Middle Selection: Read together *The Story of the Treasure Seekers*, chapter 11, "Castilian Amoroso."
Older Selection: Read together or assign as independent reading *The Fellowship of the Ring*, Book II, the first half of chapter 6, "Lothlorien."

Lesson 65

Materials Needed

- Verse Pack 1
- *Laying Down the Rails for Children*
- *Music Study with the Masters: Beethoven*
- *Five Little Peppers and How They Grew* OR *The Story of the Treasure Seekers* OR *The Fellowship of the Ring*

Book of Centuries Timeline

Book of Centuries Timeline

Scripture Memory: Work on learning a passage from Verse Pack 1 and review previously memorized verses.

Habits: Read aloud one lesson from your selected habit in *Laying Down the Rails for Children.*

Music Study: Use the Listen and Learn notes on page 42 in the *Music Study with the Masters: Beethoven* book to help you listen to and discuss *Symphony No. 5 in C Minor, Op. 67.*

> *Tip: This symphony is a very long piece; you may want to listen to it during a meal or a car trip.*

Family Read-Aloud: Continue reading your selection below.
Young Selection: Read together *Five Little Peppers and How They Grew,* chapter 5, "More Trouble."
Middle Selection: Read together *The Story of the Treasure Seekers*, chapter 12, "The Nobleness of Oswald."
Older Selection: Read together or assign as independent reading *The Fellowship of the Ring,* Book II, the last half of chapter 6, "Lothlorien."

Lesson 66

Materials Needed

- Verse Pack 1
- *Speaking [Spanish] with Miss Mason and Francois*
- *Journaling a Year in Nature*, pencils, watercolor paints, field guides
- *Five Little Peppers and How They Grew* OR *The Story of the Treasure Seekers* OR *The Fellowship of the Ring*

Scripture Memory: Work on learning a passage from Verse Pack 1 and review previously memorized verses.

Foreign Language: Work on a series from *Speaking [Spanish] with Miss Mason and Francois.*

Nature Study: Select and complete a nature study for this season from *Journaling a Year in Nature.*

Family Read-Aloud: Continue reading your selection below.
Young Selection: Read together *Five Little Peppers and How They Grew,* chapter 6, "Hard Days for Polly."
Middle Selection: Read together *The Story of the Treasure Seekers*, chapter 13, "The Robber and the Burglar."
Older Selection: Read together or assign as independent reading *The Fellowship of the Ring*, Book II, chapter 7, "The Mirror of Galadriel."

Lesson 67

Materials Needed

- Verse Pack 1
- *Singing the Great Hymns*
- *Creating a Masterpiece:* Pastels video and materials
- *Five Little Peppers and How They Grew* OR *The Story of the Treasure Seekers* OR *The Fellowship of the Ring*

Scripture Memory: Work on learning a passage from Verse Pack 1 and review previously memorized verses.

Hymn Study: Sing together all desired stanzas of "O Come, All Ye Faithful," pages 24 and 25 in *Singing the Great Hymns.*

Art: Work on a pastels project.

Family Read-Aloud: Continue reading your selection below.
Young Selection: Read together *Five Little Peppers and How They Grew,* chapter 7, "The Cloud Over the Little Brown House."
Middle Selection: Read together *The Story of the Treasure Seekers,* chapter 14, "The Divining-Rod."
Older Selection: Read together or assign as independent reading *The Fellowship of the Ring,* Book II, chapter 8, "Farewell to Lorien."

Tip: You may complete a lesson's assignments in any order that works best for your family's schedule and at any times of the day. Try to sequence lessons throughout the day to use different parts of the student's brain and body as you go along. In other words, don't schedule two "book-heavy" assignments back to back. You might put hymn singing or oral foreign language in between reading assignments, for example.

Lesson 68

Materials Needed

- Verse Pack 1
- *Laying Down the Rails for Children*
- *Picture Study Portfolio: Constable*
- Book of Centuries
- *Enjoy the Poems of Robert Louis Stevenson*; copies of selected poems
- *Five Little Peppers and How They Grew* OR *The Story of the Treasure Seekers* OR *The Fellowship of the Ring*

Scripture Memory: Work on learning a passage from Verse Pack 1 and review previously memorized verses.

Habits: Read aloud one lesson from your selected habit in *Laying Down the Rails for Children.*

Book of Centuries Timeline

Book of Centuries Timeline

John Constable, artist (1776–1837)

Picture Study: Ask students what they recall from last time's reading about Constable. Read the rest of "The Story of Constable" from *Picture Study Portfolio: Constable*, pages 13–15, and ask for an oral narration. Enter Constable in your Book of Centuries.

Poem Repetition: Give each student who can read a copy of the poem he or she has chosen from *Enjoy the Poems of Robert Louis Stevenson*. Encourage them to read through the poems on their own frequently during this term to help them learn it.

Tip: Students who cannot yet read will most likely be able to learn their poems simply by hearing it read or recited during your Poem Repetition time each week. If you would like to, you may determine another time during the week to again read the poem aloud to any non-reading student, so he can hear it twice a week.

Family Read-Aloud: Continue reading your selection below.
Young Selection: Read together *Five Little Peppers and How They Grew*, chapter 8, "Joel's Turn."
Middle Selection: Read together *The Story of the Treasure Seekers*, chapter 15, "Lo, the Poor Indian!"
Older Selection: Read together or assign as independent reading *The Fellowship of the Ring*, Book II, the first half of chapter 9, "The Great River."

Lesson 69

Materials Needed

- Verse Pack 1
- *Singing the Great Hymns*
- *Speaking [Spanish] with Miss Mason and Francois*
- *Enjoy the Poems of Robert Louis Stevenson*
- *Five Little Peppers and How They Grew* OR *The Story of the Treasure Seekers* OR *The Fellowship of the Ring*

Scripture Memory: Work on learning a passage from Verse Pack 1 and review previously memorized verses.

Hymn Study: Sing together all the stanzas of "I Sing the Mighty Power of God," pages 12 and 13 in *Singing the Great Hymns*.

Foreign Language: Work on a series from *Speaking [Spanish] with Miss Mason and Francois*.

Poetry: Read together "Pirate Story" from *Enjoy the Poems of Robert Louis Stevenson*, page 18.

Family Read-Aloud: Continue reading your selection below.

Young Selection: Read together *Five Little Peppers and How They Grew,* chapter 9, "Sunshine Again."
Middle Selection: Read together *The Story of the Treasure Seekers,* chapter 16, "The End of the Treasure-Seeking."
Older Selection: Read together or assign as independent reading *The Fellowship of the Ring*, Book II, the last half of chapter 9, "The Great River."

Lesson 70

Materials Needed

- Verse Pack 1
- *Laying Down the Rails for Children*
- *Music Study with the Masters: Beethoven*
- *Five Little Peppers and How They Grew* OR *The Story of the Treasure Seekers* OR *The Fellowship of the Ring*

Scripture Memory: Work on learning a passage from Verse Pack 1 and review previously memorized verses.

Habits: Read aloud one lesson from your selected habit in *Laying Down the Rails for Children.*

Music Study: Use the Listen and Learn notes on page 43 in the *Music Study with the Masters: Beethoven* book to help you listen to and discuss *String Quartet No. 7 in F Major, Op. 59, No. 1, "Rasumovsky."*

Tip: You can listen to your music study composer while eating lunch, running errands, sitting quietly, or getting ready for bed. Find a time that works well for your family during this season of life.

Family Read-Aloud: Continue reading your selection below.
Young Selection: Read together *Five Little Peppers and How They Grew,* chapter 10, "A Threatened Blow."
Middle Selection: Use today and tomorrow as needed to finish reading *The Story of the Treasure Seekers.*
Older Selection: Read together or assign as independent reading *The Fellowship of the Ring*, Book II, chapter 10, "The Breaking of the Fellowship."

Lesson 71

Materials Needed

- Verse Pack 1
- *Speaking [Spanish] with Miss Mason and Francois*
- *Journaling a Year in Nature*, pencils, watercolor paints, field guides
- *Five Little Peppers and How They Grew* OR *The Story of the Treasure Seekers* OR *The Fellowship of the Ring*

Book of Centuries Timeline

Book of Centuries Timeline

Scripture Memory: Work on learning a passage from Verse Pack 1 and review previously memorized verses.

Foreign Language: Work on a series from *Speaking [Spanish] with Miss Mason and Francois.*

Nature Study: Select and complete a nature study for this season from *Journaling a Year in Nature.*

Family Read-Aloud: Continue reading your selection below.
Young Selection: Read together *Five Little Peppers and How They Grew,* chapter 11, "Safe."
Middle Selection: Use today as needed to finish reading *The Story of the Treasure Seekers.*
Older Selection: Use today and tomorrow to finish reading *The Fellowship of the Ring* if needed.

Lesson 72

Materials Needed

- Verse Pack 1
- *Singing the Great Hymns*
- *Creating a Masterpiece:* Pastels video and materials
- *Five Little Peppers and How They Grew* OR *The Swiss Family Robinson* OR *The Fellowship of the Ring*

Scripture Memory: Work on learning a passage from Verse Pack 1 and review previously memorized verses.

Hymn Study: Sing together all desired stanzas of "O Come, All Ye Faithful," pages 24 and 25 in *Singing the Great Hymns.*

Art: Work on a pastels project.

Family Read-Aloud: Continue reading your selection below.
Young Selection: Read together *Five Little Peppers and How They Grew,* chapter 12, "New Friends."
Middle Selection: Read together *The Swiss Family Robinson*, chapter 1.
Older Selection: Use today to finish reading *The Fellowship of the Ring* if needed.

The Swiss Family Robinson *(1813)*

Lesson 73

Materials Needed

- Verse Pack 1
- *Laying Down the Rails for Children*
- *Picture Study Portfolio: Constable*
- *Enjoy the Poems of Robert Louis Stevenson*
- *Five Little Peppers and How They Grew* OR *The Swiss Family Robinson* OR

The Two Towers

Scripture Memory: Work on learning a passage from Verse Pack 1 and review previously memorized verses.

Habits: Read aloud one lesson from your selected habit in *Laying Down the Rails for Children.*

Be sure to take advantage of every opportunity to practice the habit your family is working on. It is the repetition that makes an action or an attitude a habit. The lessons in Laying Down the Rails for Children *are designed to help everyone focus on the habit at hand and be motivated to practice it as often as possible.*

Picture Study: Ask students what they recall from the story of Constable. Do a picture study of *Weymouth Bay* from *Picture Study Portfolio: Constable,* then discuss its Leading Thoughts on page 18 of the book.

Poem Repetition: Read aloud each selected poem from *Enjoy the Poems of Robert Louis Stevenson* and invite your students to join in on the parts they know. Encourage students to say beautiful words in a beautiful way from the beginning.

Family Read-Aloud: Continue reading your selection below.
Young Selection: Read together *Five Little Peppers and How They Grew,* chapter 13, "Phronsie Pays a Debt of Gratitude."
Middle Selection: Read together *The Swiss Family Robinson*, chapter 2.
Older Selection: Read together or assign as independent reading *The Two Towers*, Book III, chapter 1, "The Departure of Boromir."

Lesson 74

Materials Needed

- Verse Pack 1
- *Singing the Great Hymns*
- *Speaking [Spanish] with Miss Mason and Francois*
- *Enjoy the Poems of Robert Louis Stevenson*
- *Five Little Peppers and How They Grew* OR *The Swiss Family Robinson* OR *The Two Towers*

Scripture Memory: Work on learning a passage from Verse Pack 1 and review previously memorized verses.

Hymn Study: Sing together all the stanzas of "Like a River Glorious," pages 14 and 15 in *Singing the Great Hymns.*

Foreign Language: Work on a series from *Speaking [Spanish] with Miss Mason and Francois.*

Book of Centuries Timeline

Book of Centuries Timeline

Poetry: Read together "The Cow" from *Enjoy the Poems of Robert Louis Stevenson*, page 19.

Family Read-Aloud: Continue reading your selection below.
Young Selection: Use today and tomorrow to catch up on any assigned reading so far in *Five Little Peppers and How They Grew* as needed.
Middle Selection: Read together *The Swiss Family Robinson*, chapter 3.
Older Selection: Read together or assign as independent reading *The Two Towers*, Book III, the first half of chapter 2, "The Riders of Rohan."

Lesson 75

Materials Needed

- Verse Pack 1
- *Laying Down the Rails for Children*
- *Music Study with the Masters: Beethoven*
- *Five Little Peppers and How They Grew* OR *The Swiss Family Robinson* OR *The Two Towers*

Scripture Memory: Work on learning a passage from Verse Pack 1 and review previously memorized verses.

Habits: Read aloud one lesson from your selected habit in *Laying Down the Rails for Children.*

Music Study: Use the Listen and Learn notes on page 44 in the *Music Study with the Masters: Beethoven* book to help you listen to and discuss *Piano Sonata No. 14 in C-Sharp Minor, Op. 27, No. 2, (Moonlight).*

Family Read-Aloud: Continue reading your selection below.
Young Selection: Use today to catch up on any assigned reading so far in *Five Little Peppers and How They Grew* as needed.
Middle Selection: Read together *The Swiss Family Robinson*, chapter 4.
Older Selection: Read together or assign as independent reading *The Two Towers*, Book III, the last half of chapter 2, "The Riders of Rohan."

wk 1·6

Lesson 76

Materials Needed

- Verse Pack 1
- *Speaking [Spanish] with Miss Mason and Francois*
- *Journaling a Year in Nature*, pencils, watercolor paints, field guides
- *Five Little Peppers and How They Grew* OR *The Swiss Family Robinson* OR *The Two Towers*

Scripture Memory: Work on learning a passage from Verse Pack 1 and review previously memorized verses.

Book of Centuries Timeline

Foreign Language: Work on a series from *Speaking [Spanish] with Miss Mason and Francois.*

Nature Study: Select and complete a nature study for this season from *Journaling a Year in Nature.*

Family Read-Aloud: Continue reading your selection below.
Young Selection: Read together *Five Little Peppers and How They Grew,* chapter 14, "A Letter to Jasper."
Middle Selection: Read together *The Swiss Family Robinson*, chapter 5.
Older Selection: Read together or assign as independent reading *The Two Towers*, Book III, the first half of chapter 3, "The Uruk-Hai."

Lesson 77

Materials Needed

- Verse Pack 1
- *Singing the Great Hymns*
- *Creating a Masterpiece:* Pastels video and materials
- *Five Little Peppers and How They Grew* OR *The Swiss Family Robinson* OR *The Two Towers*

Scripture Memory: Work on learning a passage from Verse Pack 1 and review previously memorized verses.

Hymn Study: Sing together all desired stanzas of "O Come, All Ye Faithful," pages 24 and 25 in *Singing the Great Hymns.*

Art: Work on a pastels project.

Family Read-Aloud: Continue reading your selection below.
Young Selection: Read together *Five Little Peppers and How They Grew,* chapter 15, "Jolly Days."
Middle Selection: Read together *The Swiss Family Robinson*, chapter 6.
Older Selection: Read together or assign as independent reading *The Two Towers*, Book III, the last half of chapter 3, "The Uruk-Hai."

Lesson 78

Materials Needed

- Verse Pack 1
- *Laying Down the Rails for Children*
- *Picture Study Portfolio: Constable*
- *Enjoy the Poems of Robert Louis Stevenson*
- *Five Little Peppers and How They Grew* OR *The Swiss Family Robinson* OR *The Two Towers*

Scripture Memory: Work on learning a passage from Verse Pack 1 and review previously memorized verses.

Book of Centuries Timeline

Habits: Read aloud one lesson from your selected habit in *Laying Down the Rails for Children.*

Picture Study: Ask students what they recall about *Weymouth Bay.* Do a picture study of *The Hay Wain* from *Picture Study Portfolio: Constable,* then discuss its Leading Thoughts on page 19 of the book.

Poem Repetition: Read aloud each selected poem from *Enjoy the Poems of Robert Louis Stevenson* and invite your students to join in on the parts they know. Encourage students to take their time as they speak, not rushing through the words.

Family Read-Aloud: Continue reading your selection below.
Young Selection: Read together *Five Little Peppers and How They Grew,* chapter 16, "Getting a Christmas for the Little Ones."
Middle Selection: Read together *The Swiss Family Robinson*, chapter 7.
Older Selection: Read together or assign as independent reading *The Two Towers*, Book III, the first third of chapter 4, "Treebeard" (about 10 pages or so).

Lesson 79

Materials Needed

- Verse Pack 1
- *Singing the Great Hymns*
- *Speaking [Spanish] with Miss Mason and Francois*
- *Enjoy the Poems of Robert Louis Stevenson*
- *Five Little Peppers and How They Grew* OR *The Swiss Family Robinson* OR *The Two Towers*

Scripture Memory: Work on learning a passage from Verse Pack 1 and review previously memorized verses.

Hymn Study: Sing together all the stanzas of "To God Be the Glory," pages 16 and 17 in *Singing the Great Hymns.*

Foreign Language: Work on a series from *Speaking [Spanish] with Miss Mason and Francois.*

Poetry: Read together "Happy Thought" from *Enjoy the Poems of Robert Louis Stevenson*, page 20.

Family Read-Aloud: Continue reading your selection below.
Young Selection: Read together *Five Little Peppers and How They Grew,* chapter 17, "Christmas Bells!"
Middle Selection: Read together *The Swiss Family Robinson*, chapter 8.
Older Selection: Read together or assign as independent reading *The Two Towers*, Book III, the next third of chapter 4, "Treebeard" (about 10 pages or so).

Lesson 80

Materials Needed
- Verse Pack 1
- Book of Centuries
- *Laying Down the Rails for Children*
- *Music Study with the Masters: Beethoven*
- *Five Little Peppers and How They Grew* OR *The Swiss Family Robinson* OR *The Two Towers*

Scripture Memory: Work on learning a passage from Verse Pack 1 and review previously memorized verses.

Habits: Read aloud one lesson from your selected habit in *Laying Down the Rails for Children.*

Music Study: Read together "A Day in the Life of Beethoven" on pages 9–17 in the *Music Study with the Masters: Beethoven* book and ask for an oral narration. Enter Ludwig van Beethoven in your Book of Centuries.

Tip: Don't forget to listen to Beethoven's music sometime today or this week.

Family Read-Aloud: Continue reading your selection below.
Young Selection: Read together *Five Little Peppers and How They Grew,* chapter 18, "Education Ahead."
Middle Selection: Read together *The Swiss Family Robinson*, chapter 9.
Older Selection: Read together or assign as independent reading *The Two Towers,* Book III, the rest of chapter 4, "Treebeard."

5

Lesson 81

Materials Needed
- Verse Pack 1
- *Speaking [Spanish] with Miss Mason and Francois*
- *Journaling a Year in Nature*, pencils, watercolor paints, field guides
- *Five Little Peppers and How They Grew* OR *The Swiss Family Robinson* OR *The Two Towers*

Scripture Memory: Work on learning a passage from Verse Pack 1 and review previously memorized verses.

Foreign Language: Work on a series from *Speaking [Spanish] with Miss Mason and Francois.*

Nature Study: Select and complete a nature study for this season from *Journaling a Year in Nature.*

Book of Centuries Timeline

Ludwig van Beethoven, composer (1770–1827)

Book of Centuries Timeline

Family Read-Aloud: Continue reading your selection below.
Young Selection: Read together *Five Little Peppers and How They Grew,* chapter 19, "Brave Work and the Reward."
Middle Selection: Read together *The Swiss Family Robinson*, chapter 10.
Older Selection: Read together or assign as independent reading *The Two Towers*, Book III, the first half of chapter 5, "The White Rider."

Reminder: *Get* The Wonderful Wizard of Oz *for lesson 91 for those reading the Young Selection books.*

Lesson 82

Materials Needed

- Verse Pack 1
- *Singing the Great Hymns*
- *Creating a Masterpiece:* Pastels video and materials
- *Five Little Peppers and How They Grew* OR *The Swiss Family Robinson* OR *The Two Towers*

Scripture Memory: Work on learning a passage from Verse Pack 1 and review previously memorized verses.

Hymn Study: Sing together all desired stanzas of "O Come, All Ye Faithful," pages 24 and 25 in *Singing the Great Hymns.*

Art: Work on a pastels project.

Family Read-Aloud: Continue reading your selection below.
Young Selection: Read together *Five Little Peppers and How They Grew,* chapter 20, "Polly Is Comforted."
Middle Selection: Read together *The Swiss Family Robinson*, chapter 11.
Older Selection: Read together or assign as independent reading *The Two Towers*, Book III, the last half of chapter 5, "The White Rider."

Lesson 83

Materials Needed

- Verse Pack 1
- *Laying Down the Rails for Children*
- *Picture Study Portfolio: Constable*
- *Enjoy the Poems of Robert Louis Stevenson*
- *Five Little Peppers and How They Grew* OR *The Swiss Family Robinson* OR *The Two Towers*

Scripture Memory: Work on learning a passage from Verse Pack 1 and review previously memorized verses.

Habits: Read aloud one lesson from your selected habit in *Laying Down the Rails for Children.*

Picture Study: Ask students what they recall about *The Hay Wain.* Do a picture study of *Portrait of Maria Bicknell* from *Picture Study Portfolio: Constable,* then discuss its Leading Thoughts on page 20 of the book.

Poem Repetition: Read aloud each selected poem from *Enjoy the Poems of Robert Louis Stevenson* and invite your students to join in on the parts they know.

Family Read-Aloud: Continue reading your selection below.
Young Selection: Read together *Five Little Peppers and How They Grew,* chapter 21, "Phronsie."
Middle Selection: Read together *The Swiss Family Robinson*, chapter 12.
Older Selection: Read together or assign as independent reading *The Two Towers*, Book III, the first half of chapter 6, "The King of the Golden Hall."

Book of Centuries Timeline

Lesson 84

Materials Needed

- Verse Pack 1
- *Singing the Great Hymns*
- *Speaking [Spanish] with Miss Mason and Francois*
- *Enjoy the Poems of Robert Louis Stevenson*
- *Five Little Peppers and How They Grew* OR *The Swiss Family Robinson* OR *The Two Towers*

Scripture Memory: Work on learning a passage from Verse Pack 1 and review previously memorized verses.

Hymn Study: Sing together all the stanzas of "I Sing the Mighty Power of God," pages 12 and 13 in *Singing the Great Hymns.*

Foreign Language: Work on a series from *Speaking [Spanish] with Miss Mason and Francois.*

Poetry: Ask those students who can read to read aloud their favorite poems so far from *Enjoy the Poems of Robert Louis Stevenson.* Encourage them to speak beautiful words in a beautiful way.

Family Read-Aloud: Continue reading your selection below.
Young Selection: Read together *Five Little Peppers and How They Grew,* chapter 22, "Getting Ready for Mamsie and the Boys."
Middle Selection: Read together *The Swiss Family Robinson*, chapter 13.
Older Selection: Read together or assign as independent reading *The Two Towers*, Book III, the last half of chapter 6, "The King of the Golden Hall."

Book of Centuries Timeline

Lesson 85

Materials Needed

- Verse Pack 1
- *Laying Down the Rails for Children*
- *Music Study with the Masters: Beethoven*
- *Five Little Peppers and How They Grew* OR *The Swiss Family Robinson* OR *The Two Towers*

Scripture Memory: Work on learning a passage from Verse Pack 1 and review previously memorized verses.

Habits: Read aloud one lesson from your selected habit in *Laying Down the Rails for Children.*

Music Study: Use the Listen and Learn notes on page 45 in the *Music Study with the Masters: Beethoven* book to help you listen to and discuss *Violin Concerto in D Major, Op. 61: III. Rondo: Allegro.* Older students should also read Part 1 of "The Story of Beethoven," beginning on page 19.

Family Read-Aloud: Continue reading your selection below.
Young Selection: Read together *Five Little Peppers and How They Grew,* chapter 23, "Which Treats of a Good Many Matters."
Middle Selection: Read together *The Swiss Family Robinson*, chapter 14.
Older Selection: Read together or assign as independent reading *The Two Towers*, Book III, the first half of chapter 7, "Helm's Deep."

Lesson 86

Materials Needed

- Verse Pack 1
- *Speaking [Spanish] with Miss Mason and Francois*
- *Journaling a Year in Nature*, pencils, watercolor paints, field guides
- *Five Little Peppers and How They Grew* OR *The Swiss Family Robinson* OR *The Two Towers*

Scripture Memory: Work on learning a passage from Verse Pack 1 and review previously memorized verses.

Foreign Language: Work on a series from *Speaking [Spanish] with Miss Mason and Francois.*

Nature Study: Select and complete a nature study for this season from *Journaling a Year in Nature.*

Family Read-Aloud: Continue reading your selection below.
Young Selection: Read together *Five Little Peppers and How They Grew,* chapter 24, "Polly's Dismal Morning."
Middle Selection: Read together *The Swiss Family Robinson*, chapter 15.
Older Selection: Read together or assign as independent reading *The Two*

Book of Centuries Timeline

Towers, Book III, the last half of chapter 7, "Helm's Deep."

Lesson 87

Materials Needed

- Verse Pack 1
- *Singing the Great Hymns*
- *Creating a Masterpiece:* Pastels video and materials
- *Five Little Peppers and How They Grew* OR *The Swiss Family Robinson* OR *The Two Towers*

Scripture Memory: Work on learning a passage from Verse Pack 1 and review previously memorized verses.

Hymn Study: Sing together all desired stanzas of "O Come, All Ye Faithful," pages 24 and 25 in *Singing the Great Hymns.*

Art: Work on a pastels project.

Family Read-Aloud: Continue reading your selection below.
Young Selection: Read together *Five Little Peppers and How They Grew*, chapter 25, "Polly's Big Bundle."
Middle Selection: Read together *The Swiss Family Robinson*, chapter 16.
Older Selection: Read together or assign as independent reading *The Two Towers*, Book III, the first half of chapter 8, "The Road to Isengard."

Lesson 88

Materials Needed

- Verse Pack 1
- *Laying Down the Rails for Children*
- *Picture Study Portfolio: Constable*
- *Enjoy the Poems of Robert Louis Stevenson*
- *Five Little Peppers and How They Grew* OR *The Swiss Family Robinson* OR *The Two Towers*

Scripture Memory: Work on learning a passage from Verse Pack 1 and review previously memorized verses.

Habits: Read aloud one lesson from your selected habit in *Laying Down the Rails for Children.*

Picture Study: Ask students what they recall about *Portrait of Maria Bicknell.* Do a picture study of *Dedham Vale* from *Picture Study Portfolio: Constable,* then discuss its Leading Thoughts on page 21 of the book.

Poem Repetition: Read aloud each selected poem from *Enjoy the Poems of Robert Louis Stevenson* and invite your students to join in on the parts they know. Encourage students to enunciate clearly. If a student is leaving off final

Book of Centuries Timeline

consonant sounds (for example, a final *t* or *d* or substituting *in'* for *ing*), point out that bad habit and help him practice speaking those words correctly.

Family Read-Aloud: Continue reading your selection below.
Young Selection: Use the next three days as needed to finish any chapters of *Five Little Peppers and How They Grew.*
Middle Selection: Read together *The Swiss Family Robinson*, chapter 17.
Older Selection: Read together or assign as independent reading *The Two Towers*, Book III, the last half of chapter 8, "The Road to Isengard."

Lesson 89

Materials Needed

- Verse Pack 1
- *Singing the Great Hymns*
- *Speaking [Spanish] with Miss Mason and Francois*
- *Enjoy the Poems of Robert Louis Stevenson*
- *Five Little Peppers and How They Grew* OR *The Swiss Family Robinson* OR *The Two Towers*

Scripture Memory: Work on learning a passage from Verse Pack 1 and review previously memorized verses.

Hymn Study: Sing together all the stanzas of "Immortal, Invisible, God Only Wise," pages 18 and 19 in *Singing the Great Hymns.*

Foreign Language: Work on a series from *Speaking [Spanish] with Miss Mason and Francois.*

Poetry: Read together "Picture-Books in Winter" from *Enjoy the Poems of Robert Louis Stevenson*, page 21.

Family Read-Aloud: Continue reading your selection below.
Young Selection: Use today and tomorrow as needed to finish any chapters of *Five Little Peppers and How They Grew.*
Middle Selection: Read together *The Swiss Family Robinson*, chapter 18.
Older Selection: Read together or assign as independent reading *The Two Towers*, Book III, the first half of chapter 9, "Flotsam and Jetsam."

Lesson 90

Materials Needed

- Verse Pack 1
- *Laying Down the Rails for Children*
- *Music Study with the Masters: Beethoven*
- *Five Little Peppers and How They Grew* OR *The Swiss Family Robinson* OR *The Two Towers*

Scripture Memory: Work on learning a passage from Verse Pack 1 and review previously memorized verses.

Habits: Read aloud one lesson from your selected habit in *Laying Down the Rails for Children.*

Music Study: Use the Listen and Learn notes on page 46 in the *Music Study with the Masters: Beethoven* book to help you listen to and discuss *Piano Sonata No. 8 in C Minor, Op. 13, "Pathetique": II. Adagio cantabile.* Older students should also read Part 2 of "The Story of Beethoven," beginning on page 25.

Family Read-Aloud: Continue reading your selection below.
Young Selection: Use today to finish any chapters of *Five Little Peppers and How They Grew* as needed.
Middle Selection: Read together *The Swiss Family Robinson*, chapter 19.
Older Selection: Read together or assign as independent reading *The Two Towers*, Book III, the last half of chapter 9, "Flotsam and Jetsam."

Book of Centuries Timeline

7

Lesson 91

Materials Needed

- Verse Pack 1
- *Speaking [Spanish] with Miss Mason and Francois*
- *Journaling a Year in Nature*, pencils, watercolor paints, field guides
- *The Wonderful Wizard of Oz* OR *The Swiss Family Robinson* OR *The Two Towers*

Scripture Memory: Work on learning a passage from Verse Pack 1 and review previously memorized verses.

Foreign Language: Work on a series from *Speaking [Spanish] with Miss Mason and Francois.*

Nature Study: Select and complete a nature study for this season from *Journaling a Year in Nature.*

Family Read-Aloud: Continue reading your selection below.
Young Selection: Read together *The Wonderful Wizard of Oz*, chapter 1, "The Cyclone."
Middle Selection: Read together *The Swiss Family Robinson*, chapter 20.
Older Selection: Read together or assign as independent reading *The Two Towers*, Book III, chapter 10, "The Voice of Saruman."

Lesson 92

Materials Needed

- Verse Pack 1
- *Singing the Great Hymns*
- *Creating a Masterpiece:* Pastels video and materials

Book of Centuries Timeline

- *The Wonderful Wizard of Oz* OR *The Swiss Family Robinson* OR *The Two Towers*

Scripture Memory: Work on learning a passage from Verse Pack 1 and review previously memorized verses.

Hymn Study: Sing together all the stanzas of "Like a River Glorious," pages 14 and 15 in *Singing the Great Hymns.*

Art: Work on a pastels project.

Family Read-Aloud: Continue reading your selection below.
Young Selection: Read together *The Wonderful Wizard of Oz*, chapter 2, "The Council with the Munchkins."
Middle Selection: Read together *The Swiss Family Robinson*, chapter 21.
Older Selection: Read together or assign as independent reading *The Two Towers*, Book III, chapter 11, "The Palantir."

Lesson 93

Materials Needed

- Verse Pack 1
- *Laying Down the Rails for Children*
- *Picture Study Portfolio: Constable*
- *Enjoy the Poems of Robert Louis Stevenson*
- *The Wonderful Wizard of Oz* OR *The Swiss Family Robinson* OR *The Two Towers*

Scripture Memory: Work on learning a passage from Verse Pack 1 and review previously memorized verses.

Habits: Select a new habit to focus on. Read aloud one lesson from your selected habit in *Laying Down the Rails for Children.*

Picture Study: Ask students what they recall about *Dedham Vale.* Do a picture study of *The Cornfield* from *Picture Study Portfolio: Constable,* then discuss its Leading Thoughts on page 22 of the book.

Poem Repetition: Read aloud each selected poem from *Enjoy the Poems of Robert Louis Stevenson* and invite your students to join in on the parts they know.

Family Read-Aloud: Continue reading your selection below.
Young Selection: Read together *The Wonderful Wizard of Oz*, chapter 3, "How Dorothy Saved the Scarecrow."
Middle Selection: Read together *The Swiss Family Robinson*, chapter 22.
Older Selection: Use today to catch up on any assigned reading in *The Two Towers*, Book III, if needed.

Book of Centuries Timeline

Lesson 94

Materials Needed

- Verse Pack 1
- *Singing the Great Hymns*
- *Speaking [Spanish] with Miss Mason and Francois*
- *Enjoy the Poems of Robert Louis Stevenson*
- *The Wonderful Wizard of Oz* OR *The Swiss Family Robinson* OR *The Two Towers*

Scripture Memory: Work on learning a passage from Verse Pack 1 and review previously memorized verses.

Hymn Study: Sing together all the stanzas of "Immortal, Invisible, God Only Wise," pages 18 and 19 in *Singing the Great Hymns.*

Foreign Language: Work on a series from *Speaking [Spanish] with Miss Mason and Francois.*

Poetry: Read together "The Wind" from *Enjoy the Poems of Robert Louis Stevenson*, page 22.

Family Read-Aloud: Continue reading your selection below.
Young Selection: Read together *The Wonderful Wizard of Oz,* chapter 4, "The Road Through the Forest."
Middle Selection: Read together *The Swiss Family Robinson*, chapter 23.
Older Selection: Read together or assign as independent reading *The Two Towers*, Book IV, the first half of chapter 1, "The Taming of Smeagol."

Lesson 95

Materials Needed

- Verse Pack 1
- *Laying Down the Rails for Children*
- *Music Study with the Masters: Beethoven*
- *The Wonderful Wizard of Oz* OR *The Swiss Family Robinson* OR *The Two Towers*

Scripture Memory: Work on learning a passage from Verse Pack 1 and review previously memorized verses.

Habits: Read aloud one lesson from your selected habit in *Laying Down the Rails for Children.*

Music Study: Listen to music by Beethoven from *Music Study with the Masters: Beethoven.* Older students should also read Part 3 of "The Story of Beethoven," beginning on page 33, and give a written narration of the composer's life.

Tip: *You can listen to your music study composer while eating lunch,*

Book of Centuries Timeline

running errands, sitting quietly, or getting ready for bed. Find a time that works well for your family during this season of life.

Family Read-Aloud: Continue reading your selection below.
Young Selection: Read together *The Wonderful Wizard of Oz*, chapter 5, "The Rescue of the Tin Woodman."
Middle Selection: Use today and tomorrow as needed to catch up on any assigned chapters in *The Swiss Family Robinson.*
Older Selection: Read together or assign as independent reading *The Two Towers*, Book IV, the last half of chapter 1, "The Taming of Smeagol."

Lesson 96

Materials Needed

- Verse Pack 1
- *Speaking [Spanish] with Miss Mason and Francois*
- *Journaling a Year in Nature*, pencils, watercolor paints, field guides
- *The Wonderful Wizard of Oz* OR *The Swiss Family Robinson* OR *The Two Towers*

Scripture Memory: Work on learning a passage from Verse Pack 1 and review previously memorized verses.

Foreign Language: Work on a series from *Speaking [Spanish] with Miss Mason and Francois.*

Nature Study: Select and complete a nature study for this season from *Journaling a Year in Nature.*

Family Read-Aloud: Continue reading your selection below.
Young Selection: Read together *The Wonderful Wizard of Oz*, chapter 6, "The Cowardly Lion."
Middle Selection: Use today as needed to catch up on any assigned chapters in *The Swiss Family Robinson.*
Older Selection: Read together or assign as independent reading *The Two Towers*, Book IV, the first half of chapter 2, "The Passage of the Marshes."

Lesson 97

Materials Needed

- Verse Pack 1
- *Singing the Great Hymns*
- *Creating a Masterpiece:* Pastels video and materials
- *The Wonderful Wizard of Oz* OR *The Swiss Family Robinson* OR *The Two Towers*

Scripture Memory: Work on learning a passage from Verse Pack 1 and review previously memorized verses.

Hymn Study: Sing together all desired stanzas of "O Come, All Ye Faithful," pages 24 and 25 in *Singing the Great Hymns*.

Art: Work on a pastels project.

Family Read-Aloud: Continue reading your selection below.
Young Selection: Read together *The Wonderful Wizard of Oz*, chapter 7, "The Journey to the Great Oz."
Middle Selection: Read together *The Swiss Family Robinson*, chapter 24.
Older Selection: Read together or assign as independent reading *The Two Towers*, Book IV, the last half of chapter 2, "The Passage of the Marshes."

Lesson 98

Materials Needed

- Verse Pack 1
- *Laying Down the Rails for Children*
- *Picture Study Portfolio: Constable*
- *Enjoy the Poems of Robert Louis Stevenson*
- *The Wonderful Wizard of Oz* OR *The Swiss Family Robinson* OR *The Two Towers*

Scripture Memory: Work on learning a passage from Verse Pack 1 and review previously memorized verses.

Habits: Read aloud one lesson from your selected habit in *Laying Down the Rails for Children.*

Picture Study: Ask students what they recall about *The Cornfield.* Do a picture study of *Salisbury Cathedral from the Bishop's Garden* from *Picture Study Portfolio: Constable*, then discuss its Leading Thoughts on page 23 of the book.

Poem Repetition: Read aloud each selected poem from *Enjoy the Poems of Robert Louis Stevenson* and invite your students to join in on the parts they know. Encourage students to consider the ideas contained in the poems and think about how they can best communicate those ideas as they speak.

Family Read-Aloud: Continue reading your selection below.
Young Selection: Read together *The Wonderful Wizard of Oz*, chapter 8, "The Deadly Poppy Field."
Middle Selection: Read together *The Swiss Family Robinson*, chapter 25.
Older Selection: Read together or assign as independent reading *The Two Towers*, Book IV, chapter 3, "The Black Gate Is Closed."

Lesson 99

Materials Needed

- Verse Pack 1
- *Singing the Great Hymns*

Book of Centuries Timeline

Book of Centuries Timeline

- *Speaking [Spanish] with Miss Mason and Francois*
- *Enjoy the Poems of Robert Louis Stevenson*
- *The Wonderful Wizard of Oz* OR *The Swiss Family Robinson* OR *The Two Towers*

Scripture Memory: Work on learning a passage from Verse Pack 1 and review previously memorized verses.

Hymn Study: Sing together all the stanzas of "Immortal, Invisible, God Only Wise," pages 18 and 19 in *Singing the Great Hymns.*

Foreign Language: Work on a series from *Speaking [Spanish] with Miss Mason and Francois.*

Poetry: Read together "The Land of Nod" from *Enjoy the Poems of Robert Louis Stevenson*, page 23.

Family Read-Aloud: Continue reading your selection below.
Young Selection: Read together *The Wonderful Wizard of Oz*, chapter 9, "The Queen of the Field Mice."
Middle Selection: Read together *The Swiss Family Robinson*, chapter 26.
Older Selection: Read together or assign as independent reading *The Two Towers*, Book IV, the first half of chapter 4, "Of Herbs and Stewed Rabbit."

Lesson 100

Materials Needed

- Verse Pack 1
- *Laying Down the Rails for Children*
- *Music Study with the Masters: Beethoven*
- *The Wonderful Wizard of Oz* OR *The Swiss Family Robinson* OR *The Two Towers*

Scripture Memory: Work on learning a passage from Verse Pack 1 and review previously memorized verses.

Habits: Read aloud one lesson from your selected habit in *Laying Down the Rails for Children.*

Music Study: Use the Listen and Learn notes on page 47 in the *Music Study with the Masters: Beethoven* book to help you listen to and discuss *Piano Concerto No. 5 in E-Flat Major, Op. 73, "Emperor": III. Rondo: Allegro.*

Family Read-Aloud: Continue reading your selection below.
Young Selection: Read together *The Wonderful Wizard of Oz*, chapter 10, "The Guardian of the Gate."
Middle Selection: Read together *The Swiss Family Robinson*, chapter 27.
Older Selection: Read together or assign as independent reading *The Two Towers*, Book IV, the last half of chapter 4, "Of Herbs and Stewed Rabbit."

Lesson 101

Materials Needed

- Verse Pack 1
- *Speaking [Spanish] with Miss Mason and Francois*
- *Journaling a Year in Nature*, pencils, watercolor paints, field guides
- *The Wonderful Wizard of Oz* OR *The Swiss Family Robinson* OR *The Two Towers*

Scripture Memory: Work on learning a passage from Verse Pack 1 and review previously memorized verses.

Foreign Language: Work on a series from *Speaking [Spanish] with Miss Mason and Francois.*

Nature Study: Select and complete a nature study for this season from *Journaling a Year in Nature.*

Family Read-Aloud: Continue reading your selection below.
Young Selection: Read together *The Wonderful Wizard of Oz*, chapter 11, "The Wonderful Emerald City of Oz."
Middle Selection: Read together *The Swiss Family Robinson*, chapter 28.
Older Selection: Read together or assign as independent reading *The Two Towers*, Book IV, the first half of chapter 5, "The Window on the West."

Reminder: *Get* The Return of the King *for lesson 111 for those reading the Older Selection books.*

Book of Centuries Timeline

Lesson 102

Materials Needed

- Verse Pack 1
- *Singing the Great Hymns*
- *Creating a Masterpiece:* Pastels video and materials
- *The Wonderful Wizard of Oz* OR *The Swiss Family Robinson* OR *The Two Towers*

Scripture Memory: Work on learning a passage from Verse Pack 1 and review previously memorized verses.

Hymn Study: Sing together all the stanzas of "To God Be the Glory," pages 16 and 17 in *Singing the Great Hymns.*

Art: Work on a pastels project.

Family Read-Aloud: Continue reading your selection below.
Young Selection: Read together *The Wonderful Wizard of Oz*, chapter 12, "The Search for the Wicked Witch."

Book of Centuries Timeline

Middle Selection: Read together *The Swiss Family Robinson*, chapter 29.
Older Selection: Read together or assign as independent reading *The Two Towers*, Book IV, the last half of chapter 5, "The Window on the West."

Lesson 103

Materials Needed

- Verse Pack 1
- *Laying Down the Rails for Children*
- *Picture Study Portfolio: Constable*
- *Enjoy the Poems of Robert Louis Stevenson*
- *The Wonderful Wizard of Oz* OR *The Swiss Family Robinson* OR *The Two Towers*

Scripture Memory: Work on learning a passage from Verse Pack 1 and review previously memorized verses.

Habits: Read aloud one lesson from your selected habit in *Laying Down the Rails for Children.*

Picture Study: Ask students what they recall about *Salisbury Cathedral from the Bishop's Garden*. Do a picture study of *Seascape Study with Rain Cloud* from *Picture Study Portfolio: Constable*, then discuss its Leading Thoughts on page 24 of the book.

Poem Repetition: Read aloud each selected poem from *Enjoy the Poems of Robert Louis Stevenson* and invite your students to join in on the parts they know. Be careful you are not dictating exactly what each student's recitation should sound like. Allow for individual freedom within the boundaries of good communication. Let each child form his own relation with the poet and poem.

Family Read-Aloud: Continue reading your selection below.
Young Selection: Read together *The Wonderful Wizard of Oz*, chapter 13, "The Rescue."
Middle Selection: Read together *The Swiss Family Robinson*, chapter 30.
Older Selection: Read together or assign as independent reading *The Two Towers*, Book IV, chapter 6, "The Forbidden Pool."

Lesson 104

Materials Needed

- Verse Pack 1
- *Singing the Great Hymns*
- *Speaking [Spanish] with Miss Mason and Francois*
- *Enjoy the Poems of Robert Louis Stevenson*
- *The Wonderful Wizard of Oz* OR *The Swiss Family Robinson* OR *The Two Towers*

Scripture Memory: Work on learning a passage from Verse Pack 1 and review previously memorized verses.

Hymn Study: Sing together all the stanzas of "Immortal, Invisible, God Only Wise," pages 18 and 19 in *Singing the Great Hymns.*

Foreign Language: Work on a series from *Speaking [Spanish] with Miss Mason and Francois.*

Poetry: Invite each student to select one of the poems (or a portion of a poem) that has been read from *Enjoy the Poems of Robert Louis Stevenson* and illustrate it. Pages are provided in the back of the poetry book for illustrations. You may also create the illustration on a different sheet of paper and tuck it inside the poetry book.

> *Tip: Make sure each student signs and dates his or her drawing and notes which poem it illustrates.*

Family Read-Aloud: Continue reading your selection below.
Young Selection: Use today and tomorrow to catch up on reading any assigned chapters in *The Wonderful Wizard of Oz* as needed.
Middle Selection: Read together *The Swiss Family Robinson*, chapter 31.
Older Selection: Read together or assign as independent reading *The Two Towers*, Book IV, chapter 7, "Journey to the Cross-Roads."

Lesson 105

Materials Needed

- Verse Pack 1
- *Laying Down the Rails for Children*
- *Music Study with the Masters: Beethoven*
- *The Wonderful Wizard of Oz* OR *The Swiss Family Robinson* OR *The Two Towers*

Scripture Memory: Work on learning a passage from Verse Pack 1 and review previously memorized verses.

Habits: Read aloud one lesson from your selected habit in *Laying Down the Rails for Children.*

Music Study: Use the Listen and Learn notes on page 48 in the *Music Study with the Masters: Beethoven* book to help you listen to and discuss *Bagatelle in A Minor, WoO 59, "Fur Elise."*

Family Read-Aloud: Continue reading your selection below.
Young Selection: Use today to catch up on reading any assigned chapters in *The Wonderful Wizard of Oz* as needed.
Middle Selection: Read together *The Swiss Family Robinson*, chapter 32.
Older Selection: Read together or assign as independent reading *The Two*

Book of Centuries Timeline

Book of Centuries Timeline

10

Towers, Book IV, the first half of chapter 8, "The Stairs of Cirith Ungol."

Lesson 106

Materials Needed

- Verse Pack 1
- *Speaking [Spanish] with Miss Mason and Francois*
- *Journaling a Year in Nature*, pencils, watercolor paints, field guides
- *The Wonderful Wizard of Oz* OR *The Swiss Family Robinson* OR *The Two Towers*

Scripture Memory: Work on learning a passage from Verse Pack 1 and review previously memorized verses.

Foreign Language: Work on a series from *Speaking [Spanish] with Miss Mason and Francois.*

Nature Study: Select and complete a nature study for this season from *Journaling a Year in Nature.*

Family Read-Aloud: Continue reading your selection below.
Young Selection: Read together *The Wonderful Wizard of Oz*, chapter 14, "The Winged Monkeys."
Middle Selection: Read together *The Swiss Family Robinson*, chapter 33.
Older Selection: Read together or assign as independent reading *The Two Towers*, Book IV, the last half of chapter 8, "The Stairs of Cirith Ungol."

Lesson 107

Materials Needed

- Verse Pack 1
- *Singing the Great Hymns*
- *Creating a Masterpiece:* Pastels video and materials
- *The Wonderful Wizard of Oz* OR *The Swiss Family Robinson* OR *The Two Towers*

Scripture Memory: Work on learning a passage from Verse Pack 1 and review previously memorized verses.

Hymn Study: Sing together all desired stanzas of "O Come, All Ye Faithful," pages 24 and 25 in *Singing the Great Hymns.*

Art: Work on a pastels project.

Family Read-Aloud: Continue reading your selection below.
Young Selection: Read together *The Wonderful Wizard of Oz*, chapter 15, "The Discovery of Oz, the Terrible."
Middle Selection: Read together *The Swiss Family Robinson*, chapter 34.
Older Selection: Read together or assign as independent reading *The Two*

Towers, Book IV, chapter 9, "Shelob's Lair."

Book of Centuries Timeline

Lesson 108

Materials Needed

- Verse Pack 1
- *Laying Down the Rails for Children*
- *Picture Study Portfolio: Constable*
- *Enjoy the Poems of Robert Louis Stevenson*
- *The Wonderful Wizard of Oz* OR *The Swiss Family Robinson* OR *The Two Towers*

Scripture Memory: Work on learning a passage from Verse Pack 1 and review previously memorized verses.

Habits: Read aloud one lesson from your selected habit in *Laying Down the Rails for Children.*

Picture Study: Ask students what they recall about *Seascape Study with Rain Cloud.* Do a picture study of *Flowers in a Glass Vase* from *Picture Study Portfolio: Constable,* then discuss its Leading Thoughts on page 25 of the book.

Poem Repetition: Read aloud each selected poem from *Enjoy the Poems of Robert Louis Stevenson* and invite your students to join in on the parts they know. Help them identify any portions that they don't yet know thoroughly or could use more polish in saying aloud. Explain that they will each be asked to recite their poem over the next two weeks.

Family Read-Aloud: Continue reading your selection below.
Young Selection: Read together *The Wonderful Wizard of Oz*, chapter 16, "The Magic Art of the Great Humbug."
Middle Selection: Read together *The Swiss Family Robinson*, chapter 35.
Older Selection: Read together or assign as independent reading *The Two Towers*, Book IV, chapter 10, "The Choices of Master Samwise."

Lesson 109

Materials Needed

- Verse Pack 1
- *Singing the Great Hymns*
- *Speaking [Spanish] with Miss Mason and Francois*
- *Enjoy the Poems of Robert Louis Stevenson*
- *The Wonderful Wizard of Oz* OR *The Swiss Family Robinson* OR *The Two Towers*

Scripture Memory: Work on learning a passage from Verse Pack 1 and review previously memorized verses.

Hymn Study: Sing together all the stanzas of "Immortal, Invisible, God Only

Book of Centuries Timeline

Wise," pages 18 and 19 in *Singing the Great Hymns.*

Foreign Language: Work on a series from *Speaking [Spanish] with Miss Mason and Francois.*

Poetry: Read together "The Moon" from *Enjoy the Poems of Robert Louis Stevenson*, page 24.

Family Read-Aloud: Continue reading your selection below.
Young Selection: Read together *The Wonderful Wizard of Oz*, chapter 17, "How the Balloon was Launched."
Middle Selection: Read together *The Swiss Family Robinson*, chapter 36.
Older Selection: Use today and tomorrow to finish reading *The Two Towers* if needed.

Lesson 110

Materials Needed

- Verse Pack 1
- *Laying Down the Rails for Children*
- *Music Study with the Masters: Beethoven*
- *The Wonderful Wizard of Oz* OR *The Swiss Family Robinson* OR *The Two Towers*

Scripture Memory: Work on learning a passage from Verse Pack 1 and review previously memorized verses.

Habits: Read aloud one lesson from your selected habit in *Laying Down the Rails for Children.*

Music Study: Use the Listen and Learn notes on pages 49 and 50 in the *Music Study with the Masters: Beethoven* book to help you listen to and discuss *Symphony No. 9 in D Minor, Op. 125, "Choral": IV. Finale: Presto - Allegro assai.*

Family Read-Aloud: Continue reading your selection below.
Young Selection: Read together *The Wonderful Wizard of Oz*, chapter 18, "Away to the South."
Middle Selection: Read together *The Swiss Family Robinson,* chapter 37.
Older Selection: Use today to finish reading *The Two Towers* if needed.

Reminder: *Make sure you have the resources you will need for Term 3. See details on page 91.*

\ \

Lesson 111

Materials Needed

- Verse Pack 1

- *Speaking [Spanish] with Miss Mason and Francois*
- *Journaling a Year in Nature*, pencils, watercolor paints, field guides
- *The Wonderful Wizard of Oz* OR *The Swiss Family Robinson* OR *The Return of the King*

Scripture Memory: Work on learning a passage from Verse Pack 1 and review previously memorized verses.

Foreign Language: Work on a series from *Speaking [Spanish] with Miss Mason and Francois.*

Nature Study: Select and complete a nature study for this season from *Journaling a Year in Nature.*

Family Read-Aloud: Continue reading your selection below.
Young Selection: Read together *The Wonderful Wizard of Oz*, chapter 19, "Attacked by the Fighting Trees."
Middle Selection: Read together *The Swiss Family Robinson*, chapter 38.
Older Selection: Read together or assign as independent reading *The Return of the King*, Book V, the first third of chapter 1, "Minas Tirith" (about 10 pages or so).

Book of Centuries Timeline

Lesson 112

Materials Needed

- Verse Pack 1
- *Singing the Great Hymns*
- *Creating a Masterpiece:* Pastels video and materials
- *The Wonderful Wizard of Oz* OR *The Swiss Family Robinson* OR *The Return of the King*

Scripture Memory: Work on learning a passage from Verse Pack 1 and review previously memorized verses.

Hymn Study: Sing together all the stanzas of "I Sing the Mighty Power of God," pages 12 and 13 in *Singing the Great Hymns.*

Art: Work on a pastels project.

Family Read-Aloud: Continue reading your selection below.
Young Selection: Read together *The Wonderful Wizard of Oz*, chapter 20, "The Dainty China Country."
Middle Selection: Read together *The Swiss Family Robinson*, chapter 39.
Older Selection: Read together or assign as independent reading *The Return of the King*, Book V, the next third of chapter 1, "Minas Tirith" (about 10 pages or so).

Book of Centuries Timeline

Lesson 113

Materials Needed

- Verse Pack 1
- *Laying Down the Rails for Children*
- *Picture Study Portfolio: Constable*
- *Enjoy the Poems of Robert Louis Stevenson*
- *The Wonderful Wizard of Oz* OR *The Swiss Family Robinson* OR *The Return of the King*

Scripture Memory: Work on learning a passage from Verse Pack 1 and review previously memorized verses.

Habits: Read aloud one lesson from your selected habit in *Laying Down the Rails for Children.*

Picture Study: Ask students what they recall about *Flowers in a Glass Vase.* Use this week to catch up on any Constable picture studies from *Picture Study Portfolio: Constable.*

Poem Repetition: Ask each student who is ready to stand and recite aloud his selected poem from *Enjoy the Poems of Robert Louis Stevenson.* Help any children who need final coaching before their individual recitations next week.

Family Read-Aloud: Continue reading your selection below.
Young Selection: Read together *The Wonderful Wizard of Oz*, chapter 21, "The Lion Becomes the King of Beasts."
Middle Selection: Read together *The Swiss Family Robinson*, chapter 40.
Older Selection: Read together or assign as independent reading *The Return of the King*, Book V, the rest of chapter 1, "Minas Tirith."

Lesson 114

Materials Needed

- Verse Pack 1
- *Singing the Great Hymns*
- *Speaking [Spanish] with Miss Mason and Francois*
- *Enjoy the Poems of Robert Louis Stevenson*
- *The Wonderful Wizard of Oz* OR *The Swiss Family Robinson* OR *The Return of the King*

Scripture Memory: Work on learning a passage from Verse Pack 1 and review previously memorized verses.

Hymn Study: Sing together all the stanzas of "Immortal, Invisible, God Only Wise," pages 18 and 19 in *Singing the Great Hymns.*

Foreign Language: Work on a series from *Speaking [Spanish] with Miss Mason and Francois.*

Poetry: Read together "The Hayloft" from *Enjoy the Poems of Robert Louis Stevenson*, page 25.

Family Read-Aloud: Continue reading your selection below.
Young Selection: Read together *The Wonderful Wizard of Oz*, chapter 22, "The Country of the Quadlings."
Middle Selection: Read together *The Swiss Family Robinson*, chapter 41.
Older Selection: Read together or assign as independent reading *The Return of the King*, Book V, the first half of chapter 2, "The Passing of the Grey Company."

Book of Centuries Timeline

Lesson 115

Materials Needed

- Verse Pack 1
- *Laying Down the Rails for Children*
- *Music Study with the Masters: Beethoven*
- *The Wonderful Wizard of Oz* OR *The Swiss Family Robinson* OR *The Return of the King*

Scripture Memory: Work on learning a passage from Verse Pack 1 and review previously memorized verses.

Habits: Read aloud one lesson from your selected habit in *Laying Down the Rails for Children.*

Music Study: Listen to students' favorite pieces by Beethoven from *Music Study with the Masters: Beethoven* and ask each person to tell why that piece is his or her favorite.

Family Read-Aloud: Continue reading your selection below.
Young Selection: Read together *The Wonderful Wizard of Oz*, chapter 23, "Glinda the Good Witch Grants Dorothy's Wish."
Middle Selection: Read together *The Swiss Family Robinson*, chapter 42.
Older Selection: Read together or assign as independent reading *The Return of the King*, Book V, the last half of chapter 2, "The Passing of the Grey Company."

12

Lesson 116

Materials Needed

- Verse Pack 1
- *Speaking [Spanish] with Miss Mason and Francois*
- *Journaling a Year in Nature*, pencils, watercolor paints, field guides
- *The Wonderful Wizard of Oz* OR *The Swiss Family Robinson* OR *The Return of the King*

Scripture Memory: Work on learning a passage from Verse Pack 1 and review previously memorized verses.

Book of Centuries Timeline

Foreign Language: Work on a series from *Speaking [Spanish] with Miss Mason and Francois.*

Nature Study: Select and complete a nature study for this season from *Journaling a Year in Nature.*

Family Read-Aloud: Continue reading your selection below.
Young Selection: Read together *The Wonderful Wizard of Oz*, chapter 24, "Home Again."
Middle Selection: Read together *The Swiss Family Robinson*, chapter 43.
Older Selection: Read together or assign as independent reading *The Return of the King*, Book V, the first half of chapter 3, "The Muster of Rohan."

Lesson 117

Materials Needed

- Verse Pack 1
- *Singing the Great Hymns*
- *Creating a Masterpiece:* Pastels video and materials
- *The Wonderful Wizard of Oz* OR *The Swiss Family Robinson* OR *The Return of the King*

Scripture Memory: Work on learning a passage from Verse Pack 1 and review previously memorized verses.

Hymn Study: Sing together a favorite hymn studied so far. If desired, ask a student to sing or quote his favorite stanza.

Art: Work on a pastels project.

Family Read-Aloud: Continue reading your selection below.
Young Selection: Use the next few days as needed to finish any chapters of *The Wonderful Wizard of Oz.*
Middle Selection: Read together *The Swiss Family Robinson*, chapter 44.
Older Selection: Read together or assign as independent reading *The Return of the King*, Book V, the last half of chapter 3, "The Muster of Rohan."

Lesson 118

Materials Needed

- Verse Pack 1
- *Laying Down the Rails for Children*
- *Picture Study Portfolio: Constable*
- *Enjoy the Poems of Robert Louis Stevenson*
- *The Wonderful Wizard of Oz* OR *The Swiss Family Robinson* OR *The Return of the King*

Scripture Memory: Work on learning a passage from Verse Pack 1 and review previously memorized verses.

Habits: Read aloud one lesson from your selected habit in *Laying Down the Rails for Children.*

Picture Study: Ask each student to tell about his or her favorite Constable picture. The student may describe his favorite orally, sketch the elements of it, or write a description.

Poem Repetition: Ask each student who has not already done so to recite aloud his selected poem from *Enjoy the Poems of Robert Louis Stevenson.*

Family Read-Aloud: Continue reading your selection below.
Young Selection: Use the next few days as needed to finish any chapters of *The Wonderful Wizard of Oz.*
Middle Selection: Use the next three days to finish reading *The Swiss Family Robinson* as needed.
Older Selection: Read together or assign as independent reading *The Return of the King*, Book V, the first third of chapter 4, "The Siege of Gondor" (about 10 pages or so).

Book of Centuries Timeline

Lesson 119

Materials Needed

- Verse Pack 1
- *Singing the Great Hymns*
- *Speaking [Spanish] with Miss Mason and Francois*
- *Enjoy the Poems of Robert Louis Stevenson*
- *The Wonderful Wizard of Oz* OR *The Swiss Family Robinson* OR *The Return of the King*

Scripture Memory: Work on learning a passage from Verse Pack 1 and review previously memorized verses.

Hymn Study: Sing together a favorite hymn studied so far. If desired, ask a student to sing or quote his favorite stanza.

Foreign Language: Work on a series from *Speaking [Spanish] with Miss Mason and Francois.*

Poetry: Read some of your favorite poems so far from *Enjoy the Poems of Robert Louis Stevenson.*

Family Read-Aloud: Continue reading your selection below.
Young Selection: Use today and tomorrow as needed to finish any chapters of *The Wonderful Wizard of Oz.*
Middle Selection: Use today and tomorrow to finish reading *The Swiss Family Robinson* as needed.
Older Selection: Read together or assign as independent reading *The Return of the King*, Book V, the next third of chapter 4, "The Siege of Gondor" (about 10 pages or so).

Book of Centuries
Timeline

Lesson 120

Materials Needed

- Verse Pack 1
- *Laying Down the Rails for Children*
- *Music Study with the Masters: Beethoven*
- *The Wonderful Wizard of Oz* OR *The Swiss Family Robinson* OR *The Return of the King*

Scripture Memory: Work on learning a passage from Verse Pack 1 and review previously memorized verses.

Habits: Read aloud one lesson from your selected habit in *Laying Down the Rails for Children.*

Music Study: Ask students to tell or write about any three of the compositions of Beethoven that they have listened to.

Family Read-Aloud: Continue reading your selection below.
Young Selection: Use today to finish any chapters of *The Wonderful Wizard of Oz* as needed.
Middle Selection: Use today to finish reading *The Swiss Family Robinson* as needed.
Older Selection: Read together or assign as independent reading *The Return of the King*, Book V, the rest of chapter 4, "The Siege of Gondor."

Term 3

(12 weeks; 5 lessons/week)

Term 3 Resources List

- Scripture Memory Verse Pack 1
- Book of Centuries (one per family and older student)
- *Handicrafts Made Simple:* Crochet DVD and materials
- *Picture Study Portfolio: Velazquez*
- *Enjoy the Poems of Robert Louis Stevenson*
- *Music Study with the Masters: Chopin*
- *Journaling a Year in Nature* (one per person), pencils, watercolor paints, field guides
- *Shakespeare in Three Steps: A Midsummer Night's Dream* (and optional The Arkangel Shakespeare audio dramatization recording)
- *Singing the Great Hymns*
- *Speaking [Spanish] with Miss Mason and Francois* (or your preferred language)
- *Laying Down the Rails for Children*

Plus Family Read-Aloud Books (Select one group.)

Young Group
- *Mr. Popper's Penguins*
- *Pinocchio*

Middle Group
- *My Side of the Mountain*
- *Treasure Island*

Older Group
- *The Return of the King*
- *Where the Red Fern Grows*
- *The Innocence of Father Brown*

Suggested Weekly Schedule

Day 1 *(approx. 1 hour)*	Day 2 *(approx. 1 hour)*	Day 3 *(approx. 1 hour)*	Day 4 *(approx. 1+ hour)*	Day 5 *(approx. 1 hour)*
• Scripture Memory (10 min.) • Music Study (10 min.) • Repetition: Poem (5 min.) • Foreign Language (15 min.) • Family Read-Aloud (20 min.)	• Scripture Memory (10 min.) • Hymn Study (5 min.) • Picture Study (10 min.) • Foreign Language (15 min.) • Family Read-Aloud (20 min.)	• Scripture Memory (10 min.) • Habits (10 min.) • Poetry (5 min.) • Shakespeare (20 min.) • Family Read-Aloud (20 min.)	• Scripture Memory (10 min.) • Hymn Study (5 min.) • Nature Study (15+ min.) • Family Read-Aloud (20 min.)	• Scripture Memory (10 min.) • Habits (10 min.) • Handicrafts (20 min.) • Family Read-Aloud (20 min.)

Book of Centuries Timeline

Lesson 121

Materials Needed

- Verse Pack 1
- *Music Study with the Masters: Chopin*
- *Enjoy the Poems of Robert Louis Stevenson*
- *Speaking [Spanish] with Miss Mason and Francois*
- *Mr. Popper's Penguins* OR *My Side of the Mountain* OR *The Return of the King*

Scripture Memory: Work on learning a passage from Verse Pack 1 and review previously memorized verses.

Music Study: Use the Listen and Learn notes on page 33 in the *Music Study with the Masters: Chopin* book to help you listen to and discuss *Waltz No. 1 in E-Flat Major, Op. 18, "Valse brilliante."*

Tip: You don't have to limit your listening to only scheduled Music Study times. Feel free to play the composer's music any time throughout the week. The more the students hear it, the more familiar it will become.

Poem Repetition: Ask each student to select another poem that has been read from *Enjoy the Poems of Robert Louis Stevenson* to learn over the next few weeks.

Tip: If it would be easier, you may assign one poem for all the children to learn instead.

Foreign Language: Work on a series from *Speaking [Spanish] with Miss Mason and Francois.*

Family Read-Aloud: Continue reading your selection below.
Young Selection: Read together *Mr. Popper's Penguins*, chapter 1, "Stillwater."
Middle Selection: Read together *My Side of the Mountain*, chapter 1, "I Hole Up in a Snowstorm."
Older Selection: Read together or assign as independent reading *The Return of the King*, Book V, chapter 5, "The Ride of the Rohirrim."

Lesson 122

Materials Needed

- Verse Pack 1
- *Singing the Great Hymns*
- *Picture Study Portfolio: Velazquez*
- *Speaking [Spanish] with Miss Mason and Francois*
- *Mr. Popper's Penguins* OR *My Side of the Mountain* OR *The Return of the King*

Book of Centuries Timeline

Scripture Memory: Work on learning a passage from Verse Pack 1 and review previously memorized verses.

Hymn Study: Sing together all the stanzas of "Crown Him with Many Crowns," pages 20–23 in *Singing the Great Hymns.*

Picture Study: Read together the first half of "The Story of Velazquez" from *Picture Study Portfolio: Velazquez*, pages 11–13, and ask for an oral narration. Be sure to show the students the portrait of Velazquez on the cover of the book.

Foreign Language: Work on a series from *Speaking [Spanish] with Miss Mason and Francois.*

Family Read-Aloud: Continue reading your selection below.
Young Selection: Read together *Mr. Popper's Penguins*, chapter 2, "The Voice in the Air."
Middle Selection: Read together *My Side of the Mountain*, chapter 2, "I Get Started on This Venture."
Older Selection: Read together or assign as independent reading *The Return of the King*, Book V, chapter 6, "The Battle of the Pelennor Fields."

Lesson 123

Materials Needed

- Verse Pack 1
- *Laying Down the Rails for Children*
- *Enjoy the Poems of Robert Louis Stevenson*
- *Shakespeare in Three Steps: A Midsummer Night's Dream*
- *Mr. Popper's Penguins* OR *My Side of the Mountain* OR *The Return of the King*

Scripture Memory: Work on learning a passage from Verse Pack 1 and review previously memorized verses.

Habits: Select a new habit to focus on. Read aloud one lesson from your selected habit in *Laying Down the Rails for Children.*

Be sure to take advantage of every opportunity to practice the habit your family is working on. It is the repetition that makes an action or an attitude a habit. The lessons in Laying Down the Rails for Children *are designed to help everyone focus on the habit at hand and be motivated to practice it as often as possible.*

Poetry: Read together "Bed in Summer" from *Enjoy the Poems of Robert Louis Stevenson*, page 26.

Shakespeare: Complete "Step 1: Read the story" of *Shakespeare in Three Steps: A Midsummer Night's Dream*, pages 7–11.

Family Read-Aloud: Continue reading your selection below.
Young Selection: Read together *Mr. Popper's Penguins*, chapter 3, "Out of the Antarctic."
Middle Selection: Read together *My Side of the Mountain*, chapter 3, "I Find Gribley's Farm."
Older Selection: Read together or assign as independent reading *The Return of the King*, Book V, chapter 7, "The Pyre of Denethor."

Book of Centuries Timeline

Lesson 124

Materials Needed

- Verse Pack 1
- *Singing the Great Hymns*
- *Journaling a Year in Nature*, pencils, watercolor paints, field guides
- *Mr. Popper's Penguins* OR *My Side of the Mountain* OR *The Return of the King*

Scripture Memory: Work on learning a passage from Verse Pack 1 and review previously memorized verses.

Hymn Study: Sing together all the stanzas of "Immortal, Invisible, God Only Wise," pages 18 and 19 in *Singing the Great Hymns.*

Nature Study: Select and complete a nature study for this season from *Journaling a Year in Nature.*

Family Read-Aloud: Continue reading your selection below.
Young Selection: Read together *Mr. Popper's Penguins*, chapter 4, "Captain Cook."
Middle Selection: Read together *My Side of the Mountain*, chapter 4, "I Find Many Useful Plants."
Older Selection: Read together or assign as independent reading *The Return of the King*, Book V, the first half of chapter 8, "The Houses of Healing."

Tip: You may complete a lesson's assignments in any order that works best for your family's schedule and at any times of the day. Try to sequence lessons throughout the day to use different parts of the student's brain and body as you go along. In other words, don't schedule two "book-heavy" assignments back to back. You might put Scripture Memory or math in between reading assignments, for example.

Lesson 125

Materials Needed

- Verse Pack 1
- *Laying Down the Rails for Children*
- *Handicrafts Made Simple: Crochet* DVD and booklet
- *Mr. Popper's Penguins* OR *My Side of the Mountain* OR *The Return of the King*

Book of Centuries Timeline

Scripture Memory: Work on learning a passage from Verse Pack 1 and review previously memorized verses.

Habits: Read aloud one lesson from your selected habit in *Laying Down the Rails for Children.*

Handicrafts: Watch session 1 of the *Handicrafts Made Simple: Crochet* DVD and shop for supplies either today or later this week.

Family Read-Aloud: Continue reading your selection below.
Young Selection: Read together *Mr. Popper's Penguins*, chapter 5, "Troubles with a Penguin."
Middle Selection: Read together *My Side of the Mountain*, chapter 5, "The Old, Old Tree."
Older Selection: Read together or assign as independent reading *The Return of the King*, Book V, the last half of chapter 8, "The Houses of Healing."

Lesson 126

Materials Needed

- Verse Pack 1
- *Music Study with the Masters: Chopin*
- *Enjoy the Poems of Robert Louis Stevenson*; copies of selected poems
- *Speaking [Spanish] with Miss Mason and Francois*
- *Mr. Popper's Penguins* OR *My Side of the Mountain* OR *The Return of the King*

Scripture Memory: Work on learning a passage from Verse Pack 1 and review previously memorized verses.

Music Study: Use the Listen and Learn notes on page 34 in the *Music Study with the Masters: Chopin* book to help you listen to and discuss *Nocturne No. 2 in E-Flat Major, Op. 9, No. 2.*

Tip: *Don't worry about saving a particular music piece for the lesson in which it is scheduled to be discussed. It might be good for the students to hear a piece a few times before they learn more details about it.*

Poem Repetition: Give each student who can read a copy of the poem he or she has chosen from *Enjoy the Poems of Robert Louis Stevenson.* Encourage them to read through the poems on their own frequently during this term to help them learn it.

Tip: *Students who cannot yet read will most likely be able to learn their poems simply by hearing it read or recited during your Poem Repetition time each week. If you would like to, you may determine another time during the week to again read the poem aloud to any non-reading student, so he can hear it twice a week.*

Foreign Language: Work on a series from *Speaking [Spanish] with Miss Mason and Francois.*

Family Read-Aloud: Continue reading your selection below.
Young Selection: Read together *Mr. Popper's Penguins*, chapter 6, "More Troubles."
Middle Selection: Read together *My Side of the Mountain*, chapter 6, "I Meet One of My Own Kind and Have a Terrible Time Getting Away."
Older Selection: Read together or assign as independent reading *The Return of the King*, Book V, chapter 9, "The Last Debate."

Book of Centuries Timeline

Lesson 127

Materials Needed

- Verse Pack 1
- *Singing the Great Hymns*
- *Picture Study Portfolio: Velazquez*
- Book of Centuries
- *Speaking [Spanish] with Miss Mason and Francois*
- *Mr. Popper's Penguins* OR *My Side of the Mountain* OR *The Return of the King*

Diego Velazquez, artist (1599–1660)

Scripture Memory: Work on learning a passage from Verse Pack 1 and review previously memorized verses.

Hymn Study: Sing together all the stanzas of "Crown Him with Many Crowns," pages 20–23 in *Singing the Great Hymns.*

Picture Study: Ask students what they recall from last time's reading about Velazquez. Read the rest of "The Story of Velazquez" from *Picture Study Portfolio: Velazquez*, pages 14–17, and ask for an oral narration. Enter Velazquez in your Book of Centuries.

Foreign Language: Work on a series from *Speaking [Spanish] with Miss Mason and Francois.*

Family Read-Aloud: Continue reading your selection below.
Young Selection: Read together *Mr. Popper's Penguins*, chapter 7, "Captain Cook Builds a Nest."
Middle Selection: Read together *My Side of the Mountain*, chapter 7, "The King's Provider."
Older Selection: Read together or assign as independent reading *The Return of the King*, Book V, chapter 10, "The Black Gate Opens."

Lesson 128

Materials Needed

- Verse Pack 1
- *Laying Down the Rails for Children*
- *Enjoy the Poems of Robert Louis Stevenson*

Book of Centuries Timeline

- *Shakespeare in Three Steps: A Midsummer Night's Dream* (and optional audio recording)
- *Mr. Popper's Penguins* OR *My Side of the Mountain* OR *The Return of the King*

Scripture Memory: Work on learning a passage from Verse Pack 1 and review previously memorized verses.

Habits: Read aloud one lesson from your selected habit in *Laying Down the Rails for Children.*

Poetry: Read together "My Ship and I" from *Enjoy the Poems of Robert Louis Stevenson*, page 27.

Shakespeare: Complete Act I, Scene 1, of *Shakespeare in Three Steps: A Midsummer Night's Dream*, pages 13–15.

Family Read-Aloud: Continue reading your selection below.
Young Selection: Read together *Mr. Popper's Penguins*, chapter 8, "Penguin's Promenade."
Middle Selection: Read together *My Side of the Mountain*, chapter 8, "What I Did About the First Man Who Was After Me."
Older Selection: Use today to catch up on any assigned reading in *The Return of the King*, Book V, if needed.

Lesson 129

Materials Needed

- Verse Pack 1
- *Singing the Great Hymns*
- *Journaling a Year in Nature*, pencils, watercolor paints, field guides
- *Mr. Popper's Penguins* OR *My Side of the Mountain* OR *The Return of the King*

Scripture Memory: Work on learning a passage from Verse Pack 1 and review previously memorized verses.

Hymn Study: Sing together all the stanzas of "Like a River Glorious," pages 14 and 15 in *Singing the Great Hymns.*

Nature Study: Select and complete a nature study for this season from *Journaling a Year in Nature.*

Family Read-Aloud: Continue reading your selection below.
Young Selection: Read together *Mr. Popper's Penguins*, chapter 9, "In the Barber Shop."
Middle Selection: Read together *My Side of the Mountain*, chapter 9, "I Learn to Season My Food."
Older Selection: Read together or assign as independent reading *The Return of the King*, Book VI, the first half of chapter 1, "The Tower of Cirith Ungol."

Book of Centuries Timeline

Lesson 130

Materials Needed

- Verse Pack 1
- *Laying Down the Rails for Children*
- *Handicrafts Made Simple: Crochet* DVD, booklet, and materials
- *Mr. Popper's Penguins* OR *My Side of the Mountain* OR *The Return of the King*

Scripture Memory: Work on learning a passage from Verse Pack 1 and review previously memorized verses.

Habits: Read aloud one lesson from your selected habit in *Laying Down the Rails for Children.*

Handicrafts: Watch session 2 of the *Handicrafts Made Simple: Crochet* DVD and practice the chain stitch.

Family Read-Aloud: Continue reading your selection below.
Young Selection: Read together *Mr. Popper's Penguins*, chapter 10, "Shadows."
Middle Selection: Read together *My Side of the Mountain*, chapter 10, "How a Door Came to Me."
Older Selection: Read together or assign as independent reading *The Return of the King*, Book VI, the last half of chapter 1, "The Tower of Cirith Ungol."

Lesson 131

Materials Needed

- Verse Pack 1
- *Music Study with the Masters: Chopin*
- *Enjoy the Poems of Robert Louis Stevenson*
- *Speaking [Spanish] with Miss Mason and Francois*
- *Mr. Popper's Penguins* OR *My Side of the Mountain* OR *The Return of the King*

Scripture Memory: Work on learning a passage from Verse Pack 1 and review previously memorized verses.

Music Study: Use the Listen and Learn notes on page 35 in the *Music Study with the Masters: Chopin* book to help you listen to and discuss *Mazurka No. 13 in A Minor, Op. 17, No. 4.*

Poem Repetition: Read aloud each selected poem from *Enjoy the Poems of Robert Louis Stevenson* and invite your students to join in on the parts they know. Encourage students to say beautiful words in a beautiful way from the beginning.

Foreign Language: Work on a series from *Speaking [Spanish] with Miss Mason and Francois.*

Family Read-Aloud: Continue reading your selection below.

Book of Centuries Timeline

Young Selection: Read together *Mr. Popper's Penguins*, chapter 11, "Greta."
Middle Selection: Read together *My Side of the Mountain*, chapter 11, "Frightful Learns Her ABC's."
Older Selection: Read together or assign as independent reading *The Return of the King*, Book VI, the first half of chapter 2, "The Land of Shadow."

Lesson 132

Materials Needed

- Verse Pack 1
- *Singing the Great Hymns*
- *Picture Study Portfolio: Velazquez*
- *Speaking [Spanish] with Miss Mason and Francois*
- *Mr. Popper's Penguins* OR *My Side of the Mountain* OR *The Return of the King*

Scripture Memory: Work on learning a passage from Verse Pack 1 and review previously memorized verses.

Hymn Study: Sing together all the stanzas of "Crown Him with Many Crowns," pages 20–23 in *Singing the Great Hymns*.

Picture Study: Ask students what they recall from the story of Velazquez. Do a picture study of *Las Meninas* from *Picture Study Portfolio: Velazquez*, then discuss its Leading Thoughts on page 20 of the book.

Foreign Language: Work on a series from *Speaking [Spanish] with Miss Mason and Francois*.

Family Read-Aloud: Continue reading your selection below.
Young Selection: Read together *Mr. Popper's Penguins*, chapter 12, "More Mouths to Feed."
Middle Selection: Read together *My Side of the Mountain*, chapter 12, "I Find a Real Live Man."
Older Selection: Read together or assign as independent reading *The Return of the King*, Book VI, the last half of chapter 2, "The Land of Shadow."

Reminder: Get Pinocchio *for lesson 142 for those reading the Young Selection books.*

Lesson 133

Materials Needed

- Verse Pack 1
- *Laying Down the Rails for Children*
- *Enjoy the Poems of Robert Louis Stevenson*
- *Shakespeare in Three Steps: A Midsummer Night's Dream* (and optional audio recording)

- *Mr. Popper's Penguins* OR *My Side of the Mountain* OR *The Return of the King*

Scripture Memory: Work on learning a passage from Verse Pack 1 and review previously memorized verses.

Habits: Read aloud one lesson from your selected habit in *Laying Down the Rails for Children.*

Poetry: Read together "The Lamplighter" from *Enjoy the Poems of Robert Louis Stevenson*, page 28.

Shakespeare: Complete Act I, Scene 2, of *Shakespeare in Three Steps: A Midsummer Night's Dream*, pages 16 and 17.

Family Read-Aloud: Continue reading your selection below.
Young Selection: Read together *Mr. Popper's Penguins*, chapter 13, "Money Worries."
Middle Selection: Read together *My Side of the Mountain*, chapter 13, "The Autumn Provides Food and Loneliness."
Older Selection: Read together or assign as independent reading *The Return of the King*, Book VI, the first half of chapter 3, "Mount Doom."

Book of Centuries Timeline

Lesson 134

Materials Needed

- Verse Pack 1
- *Singing the Great Hymns*
- *Journaling a Year in Nature*, pencils, watercolor paints, field guides
- *Mr. Popper's Penguins* OR *My Side of the Mountain* OR *The Return of the King*

Scripture Memory: Work on learning a passage from Verse Pack 1 and review previously memorized verses.

Hymn Study: Sing together all the stanzas of "Immortal, Invisible, God Only Wise," pages 18 and 19 in *Singing the Great Hymns.*

Nature Study: Select and complete a nature study for this season from *Journaling a Year in Nature.*

Family Read-Aloud: Continue reading your selection below.
Young Selection: Read together *Mr. Popper's Penguins*, chapter 14, "Mr. Greenbaum."
Middle Selection: Read together *My Side of the Mountain*, chapter 14, "We All Learn About Halloween."
Older Selection: Read together or assign as independent reading *The Return of the King*, Book VI, the last half of chapter 3, "Mount Doom."

Reminder: *Get* Treasure Island *for lesson 144 for those reading the Middle Selection books.*

Book of Centuries Timeline

Lesson 135

Materials Needed

- Verse Pack 1
- *Laying Down the Rails for Children*
- *Handicrafts Made Simple: Crochet* DVD, booklet, and materials
- *Mr. Popper's Penguins* OR *My Side of the Mountain* OR *The Return of the King*

Scripture Memory: Work on learning a passage from Verse Pack 1 and review previously memorized verses.

Habits: Read aloud one lesson from your selected habit in *Laying Down the Rails for Children.*

Handicrafts: Watch session 3 of the *Handicrafts Made Simple: Crochet* DVD and practice the single crochet stitch.

Family Read-Aloud: Continue reading your selection below.
Young Selection: Read together *Mr. Popper's Penguins*, chapter 15, "Popper's Performing Penguins."
Middle Selection: Read together *My Side of the Mountain*, chapter 15, "I Find Out What to Do with Hunters."
Older Selection: Read together or assign as independent reading *The Return of the King*, Book VI, chapter 4, "The Field of Cormallen."

Lesson 136

Materials Needed

- Verse Pack 1
- Book of Centuries
- *Music Study with the Masters: Chopin*
- *Enjoy the Poems of Robert Louis Stevenson*
- *Speaking [Spanish] with Miss Mason and Francois*
- *Mr. Popper's Penguins* OR *My Side of the Mountain* OR *The Return of the King*

Frederic Chopin, composer (1800–1849)

Scripture Memory: Work on learning a passage from Verse Pack 1 and review previously memorized verses.

Music Study: Read together "A Day in the Life of Chopin" on pages 9–14 in the *Music Study with the Masters: Chopin* book and ask for an oral narration. Enter Frederic Chopin in your Book of Centuries.

Tip: *Don't forget to listen to Chopin's music sometime today or this week.*

Poem Repetition: Read aloud each selected poem from *Enjoy the Poems of Robert Louis Stevenson* and invite your students to join in on the parts they know. Encourage students to take their time as they speak, not rushing through the words.

Foreign Language: Work on a series from *Speaking [Spanish] with Miss Mason and Francois.*

Family Read-Aloud: Continue reading your selection below.
Young Selection: Read together *Mr. Popper's Penguins*, chapter 16, "On the Road."
Middle Selection: Read together *My Side of the Mountain*, chapter 16, "Trouble Begins."
Older Selection: Read together or assign as independent reading *The Return of the King*, Book VI, the first half of chapter 5, "The Steward and the King."

Lesson 137

Materials Needed

- Verse Pack 1
- *Singing the Great Hymns*
- *Picture Study Portfolio: Velazquez*
- *Speaking [Spanish] with Miss Mason and Francois*
- *Mr. Popper's Penguins* OR *My Side of the Mountain* OR *The Return of the King*

Scripture Memory: Work on learning a passage from Verse Pack 1 and review previously memorized verses.

Hymn Study: Sing together all the stanzas of "Crown Him with Many Crowns," pages 20–23 in *Singing the Great Hymns.*

Picture Study: Ask students what they recall about *Las Meninas*. Do a picture study of *The Surrender of Breda* from *Picture Study Portfolio: Velazquez*, then discuss its Leading Thoughts on page 21 of the book.

Foreign Language: Work on a series from *Speaking [Spanish] with Miss Mason and Francois.*

Family Read-Aloud: Continue reading your selection below.
Young Selection: Read together *Mr. Popper's Penguins*, chapter 17, "Fame."
Middle Selection: Read together *My Side of the Mountain*, chapter 17, "I Pile Up Wood and Go on with Winter."
Older Selection: Read together or assign as independent reading *The Return of the King*, Book VI, the last half of chapter 5, "The Steward and the King."

Reminder: *Get* Where the Red Fern Grows *for lesson 147 for those reading the Older Selection books.*

Lesson 138

Materials Needed

- Verse Pack 1

Book of Centuries Timeline

Book of Centuries Timeline

- *Laying Down the Rails for Children*
- *Enjoy the Poems of Robert Louis Stevenson*
- *Shakespeare in Three Steps: A Midsummer Night's Dream* (and optional audio recording)
- *Mr. Popper's Penguins* OR *My Side of the Mountain* OR *The Return of the King*

Scripture Memory: Work on learning a passage from Verse Pack 1 and review previously memorized verses.

Habits: Read aloud one lesson from your selected habit in *Laying Down the Rails for Children.*

Poetry: Read together "The Land of Counterpane" from *Enjoy the Poems of Robert Louis Stevenson*, page 29.

Shakespeare: Complete Act II, Scene 1, of *Shakespeare in Three Steps: A Midsummer Night's Dream*, pages 18–20.

Family Read-Aloud: Continue reading your selection below.
Young Selection: Read together *Mr. Popper's Penguins*, chapter 18, "April Winds."
Middle Selection: Read together *My Side of the Mountain*, chapter 18, "I Learn About Birds and People."
Older Selection: Read together or assign as independent reading *The Return of the King*, Book VI, the first half of chapter 6, "Many Partings."

Lesson 139

Materials Needed

- Verse Pack 1
- *Singing the Great Hymns*
- *Journaling a Year in Nature*, pencils, watercolor paints, field guides
- *Mr. Popper's Penguins* OR *My Side of the Mountain* OR *The Return of the King*

Scripture Memory: Work on learning a passage from Verse Pack 1 and review previously memorized verses.

Hymn Study: Sing together all the stanzas of "To God Be the Glory," pages 16 and 17 in *Singing the Great Hymns.*

Nature Study: Select and complete a nature study for this season from *Journaling a Year in Nature.*

Family Read-Aloud: Continue reading your selection below.
Young Selection: Read together *Mr. Popper's Penguins*, chapter 19, "Admiral Drake."
Middle Selection: Read together *My Side of the Mountain*, chapter 19, "I Have a Good Look at Winter and Find Spring in the Snow."
Older Selection: Read together or assign as independent reading *The Return*

of the King, Book VI, the last half of chapter 6, "Many Partings."

Book of Centuries Timeline

Lesson 140

Materials Needed

- Verse Pack 1
- *Laying Down the Rails for Children*
- *Handicrafts Made Simple: Crochet* DVD, booklet, and materials
- *Mr. Popper's Penguins* OR *My Side of the Mountain* OR *The Return of the King*

Scripture Memory: Work on learning a passage from Verse Pack 1 and review previously memorized verses.

Habits: Read aloud one lesson from your selected habit in *Laying Down the Rails for Children.*

Handicrafts: Watch session 4 of the *Handicrafts Made Simple: Crochet* DVD and crochet the pot holder.

Family Read-Aloud: Continue reading your selection below.
Young Selection: Read together *Mr. Popper's Penguins*, chapter 20, "Farewell, Mr. Popper."
Middle Selection: Read together *My Side of the Mountain*, chapter 20, "The Spring in the Winter and the Beginning of My Story's End."
Older Selection: Read together or assign as independent reading *The Return of the King*, Book VI, chapter 7, "Homeward Bound."

Lesson 141

Materials Needed

- Verse Pack 1
- *Music Study with the Masters: Chopin*
- *Enjoy the Poems of Robert Louis Stevenson*
- *Speaking [Spanish] with Miss Mason and Francois*
- *Mr. Popper's Penguins* OR *My Side of the Mountain* OR *The Return of the King*

Scripture Memory: Work on learning a passage from Verse Pack 1 and review previously memorized verses.

Music Study: Use the Listen and Learn notes on page 36 in the *Music Study with the Masters: Chopin* book to help you listen to and discuss *Waltz No. 6 in D-Flat Major, Op. 64, No. 1, "Minute."* Older students should also read Part 1 of "The Story of Chopin," beginning on page 15.

Poem Repetition: Read aloud each selected poem from *Enjoy the Poems of Robert Louis Stevenson* and invite your students to join in on the parts they know.

Book of Centuries Timeline

Foreign Language: Work on a series from *Speaking [Spanish] with Miss Mason and Francois.*

Family Read-Aloud: Continue reading your selection below.
Young Selection: Use today to finish reading *Mr. Popper's Penguins* as needed.
Middle Selection: Read together *My Side of the Mountain*, chapter 21, "I Cooperate with the Ending."
Older Selection: Read together or assign as independent reading *The Return of the King*, Book VI, the first third of chapter 8, "The Scouring of the Shire" (about 10 pages or so).

Lesson 142

Materials Needed

- Verse Pack 1
- *Singing the Great Hymns*
- *Picture Study Portfolio: Velazquez*
- *Speaking [Spanish] with Miss Mason and Francois*
- *Pinocchio* OR *My Side of the Mountain* OR *The Return of the King*

Scripture Memory: Work on learning a passage from Verse Pack 1 and review previously memorized verses.

Hymn Study: Sing together all the stanzas of "Crown Him with Many Crowns," pages 20–23 in *Singing the Great Hymns.*

Picture Study: Ask students what they recall about *The Surrender of Breda.* Do a picture study of *Portrait of Philip IV* from *Picture Study Portfolio: Velazquez,* then discuss its Leading Thoughts on page 22 of the book.

Foreign Language: Work on a series from *Speaking [Spanish] with Miss Mason and Francois.*

Family Read-Aloud: Continue reading your selection below.
Young Selection: Read together *Pinocchio*, chapter 1, "The Piece of Wood That Laughed and Cried Like a Child."
Middle Selection: Read together *My Side of the Mountain*, chapter 22, "The City Comes to Me."
Older Selection: Read together or assign as independent reading *The Return of the King*, Book VI, the next third of chapter 8, "The Scouring of the Shire" (about 10 pages or so).

Lesson 143

Materials Needed

- Verse Pack 1
- *Laying Down the Rails for Children*
- *Enjoy the Poems of Robert Louis Stevenson*

- *Shakespeare in Three Steps: A Midsummer Night's Dream* (and optional audio recording)
- *Pinocchio* OR *My Side of the Mountain* OR *The Return of the King*

Scripture Memory: Work on learning a passage from Verse Pack 1 and review previously memorized verses.

Habits: Read aloud one lesson from your selected habit in *Laying Down the Rails for Children.*

Poetry: Ask those students who can read to read aloud their favorite poems so far from *Enjoy the Poems of Robert Louis Stevenson*. Encourage them to speak beautiful words in a beautiful way.

Shakespeare: Complete Act II, Scene 2, of *Shakespeare in Three Steps: A Midsummer Night's Dream*, pages 21 and 22.

Family Read-Aloud: Continue reading your selection below.
Young Selection: Read together *Pinocchio*, chapter 2, "Master Cherry Gives the Wood Away."
Middle Selection: Use today as needed to finish reading *My Side of the Mountain.*
Older Selection: Read together or assign as independent reading *The Return of the King*, Book VI, the rest of chapter 8, "The Scouring of the Shire."

Lesson 144

Materials Needed

- Verse Pack 1
- *Singing the Great Hymns*
- *Journaling a Year in Nature*, pencils, watercolor paints, field guides
- *Pinocchio* OR *Treasure Island* OR *The Return of the King*

Scripture Memory: Work on learning a passage from Verse Pack 1 and review previously memorized verses.

Hymn Study: Sing together all desired stanzas of "O Come, All Ye Faithful," pages 24 and 25 in *Singing the Great Hymns.*

Nature Study: Select and complete a nature study for this season from *Journaling a Year in Nature.*

Family Read-Aloud: Continue reading your selection below.
Young Selection: Read together *Pinocchio*, chapter 3, "Geppetto Names His Puppet Pinocchio."
Middle Selection: Read together *Treasure Island*, chapter 1, "The Old Sea Dog at the Admiral Benbow."
Older Selection: Read together or assign as independent reading *The Return of the King*, Book VI, chapter 9, "The Grey Havens."

Book of Centuries Timeline

Book of Centuries
Timeline

Lesson 145

Materials Needed

- Verse Pack 1
- *Laying Down the Rails for Children*
- *Handicrafts Made Simple: Crochet* DVD, booklet, and materials
- *Pinocchio* OR *Treasure Island* OR *The Return of the King*

Scripture Memory: Work on learning a passage from Verse Pack 1 and review previously memorized verses.

Habits: Read aloud one lesson from your selected habit in *Laying Down the Rails for Children.*

Handicrafts: Watch session 5 of the *Handicrafts Made Simple: Crochet* DVD and begin to crochet the scarf.

Family Read-Aloud: Continue reading your selection below.
Young Selection: Read together *Pinocchio*, chapter 4, "The Talking-Cricket Scolds Pinocchio."
Middle Selection: Read together *Treasure Island*, chapter 2, "Black Dog Appears and Disappears."
Older Selection: Use today and tomorrow to finish reading *The Return of the King* if needed.

Lesson 146

Materials Needed

- Verse Pack 1
- *Music Study with the Masters: Chopin*
- *Enjoy the Poems of Robert Louis Stevenson*
- *Speaking [Spanish] with Miss Mason and Francois*
- *Pinocchio* OR *Treasure Island* OR *The Return of the King*

Scripture Memory: Work on learning a passage from Verse Pack 1 and review previously memorized verses.

Music Study: Use the Listen and Learn notes on page 37 in the *Music Study with the Masters: Chopin* book to help you listen to and discuss *Prelude No. 15 in D-Flat Major, Op. 28, No. 15, "Raindrop."* Older students should also read Part 2 of "The Story of Chopin," beginning on page 20.

Poem Repetition: Read aloud each selected poem from *Enjoy the Poems of Robert Louis Stevenson* and invite your students to join in on the parts they know. Encourage students to enunciate clearly. If a student is leaving off final consonant sounds (for example, a final *t* or *d* or substituting *in'* for *ing*), point out that bad habit and help him practice speaking those words correctly.

Foreign Language: Work on a series from *Speaking [Spanish] with Miss Mason and Francois.*

Family Read-Aloud: Continue reading your selection below.
Young Selection: Read together *Pinocchio*, chapter 5, "The Flying Egg."
Middle Selection: Read together *Treasure Island*, chapter 3, "The Black Spot."
Older Selection: Use today to finish reading *The Return of the King* if needed.

Book of Centuries Timeline

Lesson 147

Materials Needed

- Verse Pack 1
- *Singing the Great Hymns*
- *Picture Study Portfolio: Velazquez*
- *Speaking [Spanish] with Miss Mason and Francois*
- *Pinocchio* OR *Treasure Island* OR *Where the Red Fern Grows*

Scripture Memory: Work on learning a passage from Verse Pack 1 and review previously memorized verses.

Hymn Study: Sing together all the stanzas of "Crown Him with Many Crowns," pages 20–23 in *Singing the Great Hymns.*

Picture Study: Ask students what they recall about *Portrait of Philip IV.* Do a picture study of *The Waterseller of Seville* from *Picture Study Portfolio: Velazquez,* then discuss its Leading Thoughts on page 22 of the book.

Foreign Language: Work on a series from *Speaking [Spanish] with Miss Mason and Francois.*

Family Read-Aloud: Continue reading your selection below.
Young Selection: Read together *Pinocchio*, chapter 6, "Pinocchio's Feet Burn to Cinders."
Middle Selection: Read together *Treasure Island*, chapter 4, "The Sea-Chest."
Older Selection: Read together or assign as independent reading *Where the Red Fern Grows*, chapter 1.

Lesson 148

Materials Needed

- Verse Pack 1
- *Laying Down the Rails for Children*
- *Enjoy the Poems of Robert Louis Stevenson*
- *Shakespeare in Three Steps: A Midsummer Night's Dream* (and optional audio recording)
- *Pinocchio* OR *Treasure Island* OR *Where the Red Fern Grows*

Scripture Memory: Work on learning a passage from Verse Pack 1 and review previously memorized verses.

Habits: Read aloud one lesson from your selected habit in *Laying Down the Rails for Children.*

Book of Centuries Timeline

Poetry: Read together "A Visit from the Sea" from *Enjoy the Poems of Robert Louis Stevenson*, page 30.

Shakespeare: Complete Act III, Scene 1, of *Shakespeare in Three Steps: A Midsummer Night's Dream*, pages 23 and 24.

Family Read-Aloud: Continue reading your selection below.
Young Selection: Read together *Pinocchio*, chapter 7, "Geppetto Gives His Own Breakfast to Pinocchio."
Middle Selection: Read together *Treasure Island*, chapter 5, "The Last of the Blind Man."
Older Selection: Read together or assign as independent reading *Where the Red Fern Grows*, chapter 2.

Lesson 149

Materials Needed

- Verse Pack 1
- *Singing the Great Hymns*
- *Journaling a Year in Nature*, pencils, watercolor paints, field guides
- *Pinocchio* OR *Treasure Island* OR *Where the Red Fern Grows*

Scripture Memory: Work on learning a passage from Verse Pack 1 and review previously memorized verses.

Hymn Study: Sing together all the stanzas of "Immortal, Invisible, God Only Wise," pages 18 and 19 in *Singing the Great Hymns*.

Nature Study: Select and complete a nature study for this season from *Journaling a Year in Nature*.

Family Read-Aloud: Continue reading your selection below.
Young Selection: Read together *Pinocchio*, chapter 8, "Geppetto Makes Pinocchio New Feet."
Middle Selection: Read together *Treasure Island*, chapter 6, "The Captain's Papers."
Older Selection: Read together or assign as independent reading *Where the Red Fern Grows*, chapter 3.

Lesson 150

Materials Needed

- Verse Pack 1
- *Laying Down the Rails for Children*
- Crochet materials
- *Pinocchio* OR *Treasure Island* OR *Where the Red Fern Grows*

Scripture Memory: Work on learning a passage from Verse Pack 1 and review previously memorized verses.

Book of Centuries Timeline

Habits: Read aloud one lesson from your selected habit in *Laying Down the Rails for Children.*

Handicrafts: Finish crocheting the scarf.

Family Read-Aloud: Continue reading your selection below.
Young Selection: Read together *Pinocchio*, chapter 9, "Pinocchio Goes to See a Puppet-Show."
Middle Selection: Read together *Treasure Island*, chapter 7, "I Go to Bristol."
Older Selection: Read together or assign as independent reading *Where the Red Fern Grows*, chapter 4.

Lesson 151

Materials Needed

- Verse Pack 1
- *Music Study with the Masters: Chopin*
- *Enjoy the Poems of Robert Louis Stevenson*
- *Speaking [Spanish] with Miss Mason and Francois*
- *Pinocchio* OR *Treasure Island* OR *Where the Red Fern Grows*

Scripture Memory: Work on learning a passage from Verse Pack 1 and review previously memorized verses.

Music Study: Listen to music by Chopin from *Music Study with the Masters: Chopin*. Older students should also read Part 3 of "The Story of Chopin," beginning on page 26, and give a written narration of the composer's life.

Tip: You can listen to your music study composer while eating lunch, running errands, sitting quietly, or getting ready for bed. Find a time that works well for your family during this season of life.

Poem Repetition: Read aloud each selected poem from *Enjoy the Poems of Robert Louis Stevenson* and invite your students to join in on the parts they know.

Foreign Language: Work on a series from *Speaking [Spanish] with Miss Mason and Francois.*

Family Read-Aloud: Continue reading your selection below.
Young Selection: Read together *Pinocchio*, chapter 10, "The Puppets Recognize Their Brother Pinocchio."
Middle Selection: Read together *Treasure Island*, chapter 8, "At the Sign of the Spy-Glass."
Older Selection: Read together or assign as independent reading *Where the Red Fern Grows*, chapter 5.

Book of Centuries Timeline

Lesson 152

Materials Needed
- Verse Pack 1
- *Singing the Great Hymns*
- *Picture Study Portfolio: Velazquez*
- *Speaking [Spanish] with Miss Mason and Francois*
- *Pinocchio* OR *Treasure Island* OR *Where the Red Fern Grows*

Scripture Memory: Work on learning a passage from Verse Pack 1 and review previously memorized verses.

Hymn Study: Sing together all the stanzas of "Crown Him with Many Crowns," pages 20–23 in *Singing the Great Hymns.*

Picture Study: Ask students what they recall about *The Waterseller of Seville.* Do a picture study of *Juan de Pareja* from *Picture Study Portfolio: Velazquez,* then discuss its Leading Thoughts on page 23 of the book.

Foreign Language: Work on a series from *Speaking [Spanish] with Miss Mason and Francois.*

Family Read-Aloud: Continue reading your selection below.
Young Selection: Read together *Pinocchio,* chapter 11, "Fire-Eater Sneezes and Pardons Pinocchio."
Middle Selection: Read together *Treasure Island,* chapter 9, "Powder and Arms."
Older Selection: Read together or assign as independent reading *Where the Red Fern Grows,* chapter 6.

Lesson 153

Materials Needed
- Verse Pack 1
- *Laying Down the Rails for Children*
- *Enjoy the Poems of Robert Louis Stevenson*
- *Shakespeare in Three Steps: A Midsummer Night's Dream* (and optional audio recording)
- *Pinocchio* OR *Treasure Island* OR *Where the Red Fern Grows*

Scripture Memory: Work on learning a passage from Verse Pack 1 and review previously memorized verses.

Habits: Select a new habit to focus on. Read aloud one lesson from your selected habit in *Laying Down the Rails for Children.*

Poetry: Read together "The Sun's Travels" from *Enjoy the Poems of Robert Louis Stevenson,* page 31.

Shakespeare: Complete Act III, Scene 2, of *Shakespeare in Three Steps: A Midsummer Night's Dream,* pages 25 and 26.

Family Read-Aloud: Continue reading your selection below.
Young Selection: Read together *Pinocchio*, chapter 12, "Pinocchio Receives a Present of Five Gold Pieces."
Middle Selection: Read together *Treasure Island*, chapter 10, "The Voyage."
Older Selection: Read together or assign as independent reading *Where the Red Fern Grows*, chapter 7.

Book of Centuries Timeline

Lesson 154

Materials Needed

- Verse Pack 1
- *Singing the Great Hymns*
- *Journaling a Year in Nature*, pencils, watercolor paints, field guides
- *Pinocchio* OR *Treasure Island* OR *Where the Red Fern Grows*

Scripture Memory: Work on learning a passage from Verse Pack 1 and review previously memorized verses.

Hymn Study: Sing together all the stanzas of "I Sing the Mighty Power of God," pages 12 and 13 in *Singing the Great Hymns*.

Nature Study: Select and complete a nature study for this season from *Journaling a Year in Nature*.

Family Read-Aloud: Continue reading your selection below.
Young Selection: Read together *Pinocchio*, chapter 13, "The Inn of the Red Craw-Fish."
Middle Selection: Read together *Treasure Island*, chapter 11, "What I Heard in the Apple Barrel."
Older Selection: Read together or assign as independent reading *Where the Red Fern Grows*, chapter 8.

Lesson 155

Materials Needed

- Verse Pack 1
- *Laying Down the Rails for Children*
- *Handicrafts Made Simple: Crochet* DVD, booklet, and materials
- *Pinocchio* OR *Treasure Island* OR *Where the Red Fern Grows*

Scripture Memory: Work on learning a passage from Verse Pack 1 and review previously memorized verses.

Habits: Read aloud one lesson from your selected habit in *Laying Down the Rails for Children*.

Handicrafts: Watch session 6 of the *Handicrafts Made Simple: Crochet* DVD and begin to crochet the hat.

Book of Centuries Timeline

Family Read-Aloud: Continue reading your selection below.
Young Selection: Read together *Pinocchio*, chapter 14, "Pinocchio Falls Among Assassins."
Middle Selection: Read together *Treasure Island*, chapter 12, "Council of War."
Older Selection: Read together or assign as independent reading *Where the Red Fern Grows*, chapter 9.

Lesson 156

Materials Needed

- Verse Pack 1
- *Music Study with the Masters: Chopin*
- *Enjoy the Poems of Robert Louis Stevenson*
- *Speaking [Spanish] with Miss Mason and Francois*
- *Pinocchio* OR *Treasure Island* OR *Where the Red Fern Grows*

Scripture Memory: Work on learning a passage from Verse Pack 1 and review previously memorized verses.

Music Study: Use the Listen and Learn notes on page 38 in the *Music Study with the Masters: Chopin* book to help you listen to and discuss *Etude No. 12 in C Minor, Op. 10, No. 12, "Revolutionary."*

Poem Repetition: Read aloud each selected poem from *Enjoy the Poems of Robert Louis Stevenson* and invite your students to join in on the parts they know. Encourage students to consider the ideas contained in the poems and think about how they can best communicate those ideas as they speak.

Foreign Language: Work on a series from *Speaking [Spanish] with Miss Mason and Francois.*

Family Read-Aloud: Continue reading your selection below.
Young Selection: Read together *Pinocchio*, chapter 15, "The Assassins Hang Pinocchio to the Big Oak."
Middle Selection: Read together *Treasure Island*, chapter 13, "How My Shore Adventure Began."
Older Selection: Read together or assign as independent reading *Where the Red Fern Grows*, chapter 10.

Lesson 157

Materials Needed

- Verse Pack 1
- *Singing the Great Hymns*
- *Picture Study Portfolio: Velazquez*
- *Speaking [Spanish] with Miss Mason and Francois*
- *Pinocchio* OR *Treasure Island* OR *Where the Red Fern Grows*

Book of Centuries Timeline

Scripture Memory: Work on learning a passage from Verse Pack 1 and review previously memorized verses.

Hymn Study: Sing together all the stanzas of "Like a River Glorious," pages 14 and 15 in *Singing the Great Hymns.*

Picture Study: Ask students what they recall about *Juan de Pareja.* Do a picture study of *Old Woman Frying Eggs* from *Picture Study Portfolio: Velazquez,* then discuss its Leading Thoughts on page 23 of the book.

Foreign Language: Work on a series from *Speaking [Spanish] with Miss Mason and Francois.*

Family Read-Aloud: Continue reading your selection below.
Young Selection: Read together *Pinocchio*, chapter 16, "The Beautiful Child Rescues the Puppet."
Middle Selection: Read together *Treasure Island*, chapter 14, "The First Blow."
Older Selection: Read together or assign as independent reading *Where the Red Fern Grows*, chapter 11.

Lesson 158

Materials Needed

- Verse Pack 1
- *Laying Down the Rails for Children*
- *Enjoy the Poems of Robert Louis Stevenson*
- *Shakespeare in Three Steps: A Midsummer Night's Dream* (and optional audio recording)
- *Pinocchio* OR *Treasure Island* OR *Where the Red Fern Grows*

Scripture Memory: Work on learning a passage from Verse Pack 1 and review previously memorized verses.

Habits: Read aloud one lesson from your selected habit in *Laying Down the Rails for Children.*

Poetry: Read together "Armies in the Fire" from *Enjoy the Poems of Robert Louis Stevenson*, page 32.

Shakespeare: Complete Act IV, Scene 1, of *Shakespeare in Three Steps: A Midsummer Night's Dream*, pages 27 and 28.

Reminder: *Make arrangements now to attend a live performance or watch a video presentation of* A Midsummer Night's Dream *when you finish hearing the script.*

Family Read-Aloud: Continue reading your selection below.

Book of Centuries Timeline

Young Selection: Read together *Pinocchio*, chapter 17, "Pinocchio Will Not Take His Medicine."
Middle Selection: Read together *Treasure Island*, chapter 15, "The Man of the Island."
Older Selection: Read together or assign as independent reading *Where the Red Fern Grows*, chapter 12.

Reminder: *Get* The Innocence of Father Brown *for lesson 168 for those reading the Older Selection books.*

Lesson 159

Materials Needed

- Verse Pack 1
- *Singing the Great Hymns*
- *Journaling a Year in Nature*, pencils, watercolor paints, field guides
- *Pinocchio* OR *Treasure Island* OR *Where the Red Fern Grows*

Scripture Memory: Work on learning a passage from Verse Pack 1 and review previously memorized verses.

Hymn Study: Sing together all the stanzas of "Crown Him with Many Crowns," pages 20–23 in *Singing the Great Hymns*.

Nature Study: Select and complete a nature study for this season from *Journaling a Year in Nature*.

Family Read-Aloud: Continue reading your selection below.
Young Selection: Read together *Pinocchio*, chapter 18, "Pinocchio Again Meets the Fox and the Cat."
Middle Selection: Read together *Treasure Island*, chapter 16, "Narrative Continued By the Doctor—How the Ship was Abandoned."
Older Selection: Read together or assign as independent reading *Where the Red Fern Grows*, chapter 13.

Lesson 160

Materials Needed

- Verse Pack 1
- *Laying Down the Rails for Children*
- Crochet materials
- *Pinocchio* OR *Treasure Island* OR *Where the Red Fern Grows*

Scripture Memory: Work on learning a passage from Verse Pack 1 and review previously memorized verses.

Habits: Read aloud one lesson from your selected habit in *Laying Down the Rails for Children*.

Handicrafts: Finish crocheting the hat.

Family Read-Aloud: Continue reading your selection below.
Young Selection: Use today as needed to catch up on any assigned chapters so far in *Pinocchio*.
Middle Selection: Read together *Treasure Island*, chapter 17, "The Jolly-Boat's Last Trip."
Older Selection: Read together or assign as independent reading *Where the Red Fern Grows*, chapter 14.

Lesson 161

Materials Needed

- Verse Pack 1
- *Music Study with the Masters: Chopin*
- *Enjoy the Poems of Robert Louis Stevenson*
- *Speaking [Spanish] with Miss Mason and Francois*
- *Pinocchio* OR *Treasure Island* OR *Where the Red Fern Grows*

Scripture Memory: Work on learning a passage from Verse Pack 1 and review previously memorized verses.

Music Study: Use the Listen and Learn notes on page 39 in the *Music Study with the Masters: Chopin* book to help you listen to and discuss *Etude No. 5 in G-Flat Major, Op. 10, No. 5, "Black Keys."*

Poem Repetition: Read aloud each selected poem from *Enjoy the Poems of Robert Louis Stevenson* and invite your students to join in on the parts they know. Be careful you are not dictating exactly what each student's recitation should sound like. Allow for individual freedom within the boundaries of good communication. Let each child form his own relation with the poet and poem.

Foreign Language: Work on a series from *Speaking [Spanish] with Miss Mason and Francois.*

Family Read-Aloud: Continue reading your selection below.
Young Selection: Read together *Pinocchio*, chapter 19, "Pinocchio Is Robbed of His Money."
Middle Selection: Read together *Treasure Island*, chapter 18, "End of the First Day's Fighting."
Older Selection: Read together or assign as independent reading *Where the Red Fern Grows,* chapter 15.

Lesson 162

Materials Needed

- Verse Pack 1
- *Singing the Great Hymns*
- *Picture Study Portfolio: Velazquez*

Book of Centuries Timeline

Book of Centuries Timeline

- *Speaking [Spanish] with Miss Mason and Francois*
- *Pinocchio* OR *Treasure Island* OR *Where the Red Fern Grows*

Scripture Memory: Work on learning a passage from Verse Pack 1 and review previously memorized verses.

Hymn Study: Sing together all the stanzas of "Immortal, Invisible, God Only Wise," pages 18 and 19 in *Singing the Great Hymns.*

Picture Study: Ask students what they recall about *Old Woman Frying Eggs.* Do a picture study of *The Adoration of the Magi* from *Picture Study Portfolio: Velazquez*, then discuss its Leading Thoughts on page 24 of the book.

Foreign Language: Work on a series from *Speaking [Spanish] with Miss Mason and Francois.*

Family Read-Aloud: Continue reading your selection below.
Young Selection: Read together *Pinocchio*, chapter 20, "Pinocchio Starts Back to the Fairy's House."
Middle Selection: Use today to catch up on any assigned chapters so far in *Treasure Island* if needed.
Older Selection: Read together or assign as independent reading *Where the Red Fern Grows*, chapter 16.

Lesson 163

Materials Needed

- Verse Pack 1
- *Laying Down the Rails for Children*
- *Enjoy the Poems of Robert Louis Stevenson*
- *Shakespeare in Three Steps: A Midsummer Night's Dream* (and optional audio recording)
- *Pinocchio* OR *Treasure Island* OR *Where the Red Fern Grows*

Scripture Memory: Work on learning a passage from Verse Pack 1 and review previously memorized verses.

Habits: Read aloud one lesson from your selected habit in *Laying Down the Rails for Children.*

Poetry: Invite each child to select one of the poems (or a portion of a poem) that has been read from *Enjoy the Poems of Robert Louis Stevenson* and illustrate it. Pages are provided in the back of the poetry book for illustrations. You may also create the illustration on a different sheet of paper and tuck it inside the poetry book.

Shakespeare: Complete Act IV, Scene 2, of *Shakespeare in Three Steps: A Midsummer Night's Dream*, pages 29 and 30.

Family Read-Aloud: Continue reading your selection below.

Young Selection: Read together *Pinocchio*, chapter 21, "Pinocchio Acts as Watch-Dog."
Middle Selection: Read together *Treasure Island*, chapter 19, "Narrative Resumed by Jim Hawkins—The Garrison in the Stockade."
Older Selection: Read together or assign as independent reading *Where the Red Fern Grows*, chapter 17.

Lesson 164

Materials Needed

- Verse Pack 1
- *Singing the Great Hymns*
- *Journaling a Year in Nature*, pencils, watercolor paints, field guides
- *Pinocchio* OR *Treasure Island* OR *Where the Red Fern Grows*

Scripture Memory: Work on learning a passage from Verse Pack 1 and review previously memorized verses.

Hymn Study: Sing together all the stanzas of "To God Be the Glory," pages 16 and 17 in *Singing the Great Hymns*.

Nature Study: Select and complete a nature study for this season from *Journaling a Year in Nature*.

Family Read-Aloud: Continue reading your selection below.
Young Selection: Read together *Pinocchio*, chapter 22, "Pinocchio Discovers the Robbers."
Middle Selection: Read together *Treasure Island*, chapter 20, "Silver's Embassy."
Older Selection: Read together or assign as independent reading *Where the Red Fern Grows*, chapter 18.

Lesson 165

Materials Needed

- Verse Pack 1
- *Laying Down the Rails for Children*
- *Handicrafts Made Simple: Crochet* DVD, booklet, and materials
- *Pinocchio* OR *Treasure Island* OR *Where the Red Fern Grows*

Scripture Memory: Work on learning a passage from Verse Pack 1 and review previously memorized verses.

Habits: Read aloud one lesson from your selected habit in *Laying Down the Rails for Children*.

Handicrafts: Watch session 7 of the *Handicrafts Made Simple: Crochet* DVD and crochet the juggling balls.

Family Read-Aloud: Continue reading your selection below.

Book of Centuries Timeline

Book of Centuries Timeline

Young Selection: Read together *Pinocchio*, chapter 23, "Pinocchio Flies to the Seashore."
Middle Selection: Read together *Treasure Island*, chapter 21, "The Attack."
Older Selection: Read together or assign as independent reading *Where the Red Fern Grows*, chapter 19.

Lesson 166

Materials Needed

- Verse Pack 1
- *Music Study with the Masters: Chopin*
- *Enjoy the Poems of Robert Louis Stevenson*
- *Speaking [Spanish] with Miss Mason and Francois*
- *Pinocchio* OR *Treasure Island* OR *Where the Red Fern Grows*

Scripture Memory: Work on learning a passage from Verse Pack 1 and review previously memorized verses.

Music Study: Use the Listen and Learn notes on page 40 in the *Music Study with the Masters: Chopin* book to help you listen to and discuss *Piano Sonata No. 2 in B-Flat Minor, Op. 35.*

Tip: This is a longer piece; you may want to listen to it during a meal.

Poem Repetition: Read aloud each selected poem from *Enjoy the Poems of Robert Louis Stevenson* and invite your students to join in on the parts they know. Help them identify any portions that they don't yet know thoroughly or could use more polish in saying aloud. Explain that they will each be asked to recite their poem over the next two weeks.

Foreign Language: Work on a series from *Speaking [Spanish] with Miss Mason and Francois.*

Family Read-Aloud: Continue reading your selection below.
Young Selection: Read together *Pinocchio*, chapter 24, "Pinocchio Finds the Fairy Again."
Middle Selection: Read together *Treasure Island*, chapter 22, "How My Sea Adventure Began."
Older Selection: Read together or assign as independent reading *Where the Red Fern Grows*, chapter 20.

Lesson 167

Materials Needed

- Verse Pack 1
- *Singing the Great Hymns*
- *Picture Study Portfolio: Velazquez*

- *Speaking [Spanish] with Miss Mason and Francois*
- *Pinocchio* OR *Treasure Island* OR *Where the Red Fern Grows*

Scripture Memory: Work on learning a passage from Verse Pack 1 and review previously memorized verses.

Hymn Study: Sing together all the stanzas of "Crown Him with Many Crowns," pages 20–23 in *Singing the Great Hymns.*

Picture Study: Ask students what they recall about Velazquez's rendition of *The Adoration of the Magi.* Do a picture study of *Aesop* from *Picture Study Portfolio: Velazquez,* then discuss its Leading Thoughts on page 24 of the book.

Foreign Language: Work on a series from *Speaking [Spanish] with Miss Mason and Francois.*

Family Read-Aloud: Continue reading your selection below.
Young Selection: Read together *Pinocchio,* chapter 25, "Pinocchio Promises the Fairy to Be Good."
Middle Selection: Read together *Treasure Island,* chapter 23, "The Ebb-Tide Runs."
Older Selection: Use today to finish reading *Where the Red Fern Grows* if needed.

Lesson 168

Materials Needed

- Verse Pack 1
- *Laying Down the Rails for Children*
- *Enjoy the Poems of Robert Louis Stevenson*
- *Shakespeare in Three Steps: A Midsummer Night's Dream* (and optional audio recording)
- *Pinocchio* OR *Treasure Island* OR *The Innocence of Father Brown*

Scripture Memory: Work on learning a passage from Verse Pack 1 and review previously memorized verses.

Habits: Read aloud one lesson from your selected habit in *Laying Down the Rails for Children.*

Poetry: Read together "Looking-Glass River" from *Enjoy the Poems of Robert Louis Stevenson,* page 33.

Shakespeare: Complete Act V of *Shakespeare in Three Steps: A Midsummer Night's Dream,* pages 31–33.

Family Read-Aloud: Continue reading your selection below.
Young Selection: Read together *Pinocchio,* chapter 26, "The Terrible Dog-Fish."
Middle Selection: Read together *Treasure Island,* chapter 24, "The Cruise of the Coracle."
Older Selection: Read together or assign as independent reading *The Innocence*

Book of Centuries Timeline

Book of Centuries Timeline

of Father Brown, chapter 1, "The Blue Cross."

Lesson 169

Materials Needed

- Verse Pack 1
- *Singing the Great Hymns*
- *Journaling a Year in Nature*, pencils, watercolor paints, field guides
- *Pinocchio* OR *Treasure Island* OR *The Innocence of Father Brown*

Scripture Memory: Work on learning a passage from Verse Pack 1 and review previously memorized verses.

Hymn Study: Sing together all desired stanzas of "O Come, All Ye Faithful," pages 24 and 25 in *Singing the Great Hymns.*

Nature Study: Select and complete a nature study for this season from *Journaling a Year in Nature.*

Family Read-Aloud: Continue reading your selection below.
Young Selection: Read together *Pinocchio*, chapter 27, "Pinocchio Is Arrested by the Gendarmes."
Middle Selection: Read together *Treasure Island*, chapter 25, "I Strike the Jolly Roger."
Older Selection: Read together or assign as independent reading *The Innocence of Father Brown*, chapter 2, "The Secret Garden."

Lesson 170

Materials Needed

- Verse Pack 1
- *Laying Down the Rails for Children*
- *Handicrafts Made Simple: Crochet* DVD, booklet, and materials
- *Pinocchio* OR *Treasure Island* OR *The Innocence of Father Brown*

Scripture Memory: Work on learning a passage from Verse Pack 1 and review previously memorized verses.

Habits: Read aloud one lesson from your selected habit in *Laying Down the Rails for Children.*

Handicrafts: Watch session 8 of the *Handicrafts Made Simple: Crochet* DVD and begin to crochet the blanket. (You will have two more weeks to finish the blanket.)

Family Read-Aloud: Continue reading your selection below.
Young Selection: Read together *Pinocchio*, chapter 28, "Pinocchio Escapes Being Fried Like a Fish."
Middle Selection: Read together *Treasure Island*, chapter 26, "Israel Hands."

Book of Centuries Timeline

Older Selection: Read together or assign as independent reading *The Innocence of Father Brown*, chapter 3, "The Queer Feet."

Lesson 171

Materials Needed

- Verse Pack 1
- *Music Study with the Masters: Chopin*
- *Enjoy the Poems of Robert Louis Stevenson*
- *Speaking [Spanish] with Miss Mason and Francois*
- *Pinocchio* OR *Treasure Island* OR *The Innocence of Father Brown*

Scripture Memory: Work on learning a passage from Verse Pack 1 and review previously memorized verses.

Music Study: Listen to students' favorite pieces by Chopin from *Music Study with the Masters: Chopin* and ask each person to tell why that piece is his or her favorite.

Poem Repetition: Ask each student who is ready to stand and recite aloud his selected poem from *Enjoy the Poems of Robert Louis Stevenson.* Help any students who need final coaching before their individual recitations next week.

Foreign Language: Work on a series from *Speaking [Spanish] with Miss Mason and Francois.*

Family Read-Aloud: Continue reading your selection below.
Young Selection: Read together *Pinocchio,* chapter 29, "He Returns to the Fairy's House."
Middle Selection: Read together *Treasure Island*, chapter 27, "Pieces of Eight."
Older Selection: Read together or assign as independent reading *The Innocence of Father Brown,* chapter 4, "The Flying Stars."

Lesson 172

Materials Needed

- Verse Pack 1
- *Singing the Great Hymns*
- *Picture Study Portfolio: Velazquez*
- *Speaking [Spanish] with Miss Mason and Francois*
- *Pinocchio* OR *Treasure Island* OR *The Innocence of Father Brown*

Scripture Memory: Work on learning a passage from Verse Pack 1 and review previously memorized verses.

Hymn Study: Sing together all the stanzas of "Immortal, Invisible, God Only Wise," pages 18 and 19 in *Singing the Great Hymns.*

Picture Study: Ask students what they recall about Velazquez's portrayal of

Book of Centuries Timeline

Aesop. Use this week to catch up on any Velazquez picture studies from *Picture Study Portfolio: Velazquez.*

Foreign Language: Work on a series from *Speaking [Spanish] with Miss Mason and Francois.*

Family Read-Aloud: Continue reading your selection below.
Young Selection: Read together *Pinocchio*, chapter 30, "The Land of Boobies."
Middle Selection: Read together *Treasure Island*, chapter 28, "In the Enemy's Camp."
Older Selection: Read together or assign as independent reading *The Innocence of Father Brown*, chapter 5, "The Invisible Man."

Lesson 173

Materials Needed

- Verse Pack 1
- *Laying Down the Rails for Children*
- *Enjoy the Poems of Robert Louis Stevenson*
- *Shakespeare in Three Steps: A Midsummer Night's Dream* (and optional audio recording)
- *Pinocchio* OR *Treasure Island* OR *The Innocence of Father Brown*

Scripture Memory: Work on learning a passage from Verse Pack 1 and review previously memorized verses.

Habits: Read aloud one lesson from your selected habit in *Laying Down the Rails for Children.*

Poetry: Read together "Winter-Time" from *Enjoy the Poems of Robert Louis Stevenson*, page 34.

Shakespeare: Use this week and next week to catch up on any portions of "Step 2: Hear the script" in *Shakespeare in Three Steps: A Midsummer Night's Dream* or to complete "Step 3: Watch the play."

Family Read-Aloud: Continue reading your selection below.
Young Selection: Read together *Pinocchio*, chapter 31, "Pinocchio Enjoys Five Months of Happiness."
Middle Selection: Read together *Treasure Island*, chapter 29, "The Black Spot Again."
Older Selection: Read together or assign as independent reading *The Innocence of Father Brown*, chapter 6, "The Honour of Israel Gow."

Lesson 174

Materials Needed

- Verse Pack 1
- *Singing the Great Hymns*

- *Journaling a Year in Nature*, pencils, watercolor paints, field guides
- *Pinocchio* OR *Treasure Island* OR *The Innocence of Father Brown*

Scripture Memory: Work on learning a passage from Verse Pack 1 and review previously memorized verses.

Hymn Study: Sing together all the stanzas of "Crown Him with Many Crowns," pages 20–23 in *Singing the Great Hymns.*

Nature Study: Select and complete a nature study for this season from *Journaling a Year in Nature.*

Family Read-Aloud: Continue reading your selection below.
Young Selection: Read together *Pinocchio*, chapter 32, "Pinocchio Turns into a Donkey."
Middle Selection: Read together *Treasure Island*, chapter 30, "On Parole."
Older Selection: Read together or assign as independent reading *The Innocence of Father Brown*, chapter 7, "The Wrong Shape."

Lesson 175

Materials Needed

- Verse Pack 1
- *Laying Down the Rails for Children*
- Crochet materials
- *Pinocchio* OR *Treasure Island* OR *The Innocence of Father Brown*

Scripture Memory: Work on learning a passage from Verse Pack 1 and review previously memorized verses.

Habits: Read aloud one lesson from your selected habit in *Laying Down the Rails for Children.*

Handicrafts: Continue to work on the blanket.

Family Read-Aloud: Continue reading your selection below.
Young Selection: Read together *Pinocchio*, chapter 33, "Pinocchio Is Trained for the Circus."
Middle Selection: Read together *Treasure Island*, chapter 31, "The Treasure Hunt—Flint's Pointer."
Older Selection: Read together or assign as independent reading *The Innocence of Father Brown*, chapter 8, "The Sins of Prince Saradine."

Lesson 176

Materials Needed

- Verse Pack 1
- *Music Study with the Masters: Chopin*
- *Enjoy the Poems of Robert Louis Stevenson*

Book of Centuries Timeline

Book of Centuries Timeline

- *Speaking [Spanish] with Miss Mason and Francois*
- *Pinocchio* OR *Treasure Island* OR *The Innocence of Father Brown*

Scripture Memory: Work on learning a passage from Verse Pack 1 and review previously memorized verses.

Music Study: Ask students to tell or write about any three of the compositions of Chopin that they have listened to.

Poem Repetition: Ask each student who has not already done so to recite aloud his selected poem from *Enjoy the Poems of Robert Louis Stevenson.*

Foreign Language: Work on a series from *Speaking [Spanish] with Miss Mason and Francois.*

Family Read-Aloud: Continue reading your selection below.
Young Selection: Read together *Pinocchio*, chapter 34, "Pinocchio Is Swallowed by the Dog-Fish."
Middle Selection: Read together *Treasure Island*, chapter 32, "The Voice Among the Trees."
Older Selection: Read together or assign as independent reading *The Innocence of Father Brown*, chapter 9, "The Hammer of God."

Lesson 177

Materials Needed

- Verse Pack 1
- *Singing the Great Hymns*
- *Picture Study Portfolio: Velazquez*
- *Speaking [Spanish] with Miss Mason and Francois*
- *Pinocchio* OR *Treasure Island* OR *The Innocence of Father Brown*

Scripture Memory: Work on learning a passage from Verse Pack 1 and review previously memorized verses.

Hymn Study: Sing together a favorite hymn studied so far. If desired, ask a student to sing or quote his favorite stanza.

Picture Study: Ask each student to tell about his or her favorite Velazquez picture. The student may describe his favorite orally, sketch the elements of it, or write a description.

Foreign Language: Work on a series from *Speaking [Spanish] with Miss Mason and Francois.*

Family Read-Aloud: Continue reading your selection below.
Young Selection: Read together *Pinocchio*, chapter 35, "A Happy Surprise for Pinocchio."
Middle Selection: Read together *Treasure Island*, chapter 33, "The Fall of a Chieftain."

Older Selection: Read together or assign as independent reading *The Innocence of Father Brown*, chapter 10, "The Eye of Apollo."

Lesson 178

Materials Needed

- Verse Pack 1
- *Laying Down the Rails for Children*
- *Enjoy the Poems of Robert Louis Stevenson*
- *Shakespeare in Three Steps: A Midsummer Night's Dream* (and optional audio recording)
- *Pinocchio* OR *Treasure Island* OR *The Innocence of Father Brown*

Scripture Memory: Work on learning a passage from Verse Pack 1 and review previously memorized verses.

Habits: Read aloud one lesson from your selected habit in *Laying Down the Rails for Children.*

Poetry: Read some of your favorite poems from *Enjoy the Poems of Robert Louis Stevenson.*

Shakespeare: Use this week to catch up on any portions of "Step 2: Hear the script" in *Shakespeare in Three Steps: A Midsummer Night's Dream* or to complete "Step 3: Watch the play."

Family Read-Aloud: Continue reading your selection below.
Young Selection: Read together *Pinocchio*, chapter 36, "Pinocchio At Last Ceases to Be a Puppet and Becomes a Boy."
Middle Selection: Read together *Treasure Island*, chapter 34, "And Last."
Older Selection: Read together or assign as independent reading *The Innocence of Father Brown*, chapter 11, "The Sign of the Broken Sword."

Lesson 179

Materials Needed

- Verse Pack 1
- *Singing the Great Hymns*
- *Journaling a Year in Nature*, pencils, watercolor paints, field guides
- *Pinocchio* OR *Treasure Island* OR *The Innocence of Father Brown*

Scripture Memory: Work on learning a passage from Verse Pack 1 and review previously memorized verses.

Hymn Study: Sing together a favorite hymn studied so far. If desired, ask a student to sing or quote his favorite stanza.

Nature Study: Select and complete a nature study for this season from *Journaling a Year in Nature.*

Book of Centuries Timeline

Book of Centuries Timeline

Family Read-Aloud: Continue reading your selection below.
Young Selection: Use today and tomorrow as needed to finish any chapters of *Pinocchio.*
Middle Selection: Use today and tomorrow as needed to finish any chapters of *Treasure Island.*
Older Selection: Read together or assign as independent reading *The Innocence of Father Brown*, chapter 12, "The Three Tools of Death."

Lesson 180

Materials Needed

- Verse Pack 1
- *Laying Down the Rails for Children*
- Crochet materials
- *Pinocchio* OR *Treasure Island* OR *The Innocence of Father Brown*

Scripture Memory: Work on learning a passage from Verse Pack 1 and review previously memorized verses.

Habits: Read aloud one lesson from your selected habit in *Laying Down the Rails for Children.*

Handicrafts: Finish crocheting the blanket.

Family Read-Aloud: Continue reading your selection below.
Young Selection: Use today as needed to finish any chapters of *Pinocchio.*
Middle Selection: Use today to finish reading *Treasure Island* if needed.
Older Selection: Use today to finish reading *The Innocence of Father Brown* if needed.

Charlotte Mason Methods Used in These Lesson Plans

Notes

Scripture Memory

Charlotte Mason's students memorized a lot of Scripture—both shorter passages and longer passages. The Verse Card Pack recommended in this book contains a variety of passages ranging from single verses to whole psalms.

The method is simply this: once or twice each day read aloud the passage you are memorizing. As the words become familiar, the family members should join in saying the parts they know. Continue the one or two readings a day until all family members can recite the Scripture together with confidence.

It doesn't matter how long the passage is. Simply once or twice each day read the entire passage through until everyone can recite it together. Don't worry about how many days it takes for everyone to memorize the selected Scripture. Hiding God's Word in your heart is not a race; it's a lifelong habit.

You will find instructions and a video at simplycm.com/scripture-memory outlining an easy-to-use system that will help you and your children review and retain hundreds of verses in just five or ten minutes a day.

Nature Study

Time outside—getting to know God's creation up close and for yourself—lays a solid foundation for science studies, cultivates a habit of close observation, and gives everyone a nice break from indoor school work. Charlotte's students spent one half-day every week in the fields, observing the changing of the seasons and becoming familiar with their local flowers, trees, birds, weather, insects, and more.

Try to get outside with the whole family at least once each week. Give every family member a nature notebook in which to record their observations. Their entries could be made as pencil sketches, written descriptions, or watercolor paintings. Encourage children to draw what they see, not what they think something should look like. Help them research to learn the names of what they see and label their entries. You can use field guides—printed or electronic—to help identify their findings.

Happily, nature study can be enjoyed your entire lives. You and your children don't have to identify everything you see all at once. Simply identify a few things each year and get to know them well. As you develop a relationship with God's creation, your knowledge and enjoyment of nature will grow.

Narration

When you ask a child to narrate, you're asking him to tell back in his own words what he just saw, heard, or read. Because the child must think through the information and determine how to present it, mixed with his own opinion and impressions, this method of evaluation requires a much higher thinking level than mere fill-in-the-blank or answer-the-posed-question-with-a-fact methods. When requesting a child to narrate, word the question in an open,

Notes

essay-type form, such as "Tell all you know about ___" or "Describe ___."

Oral Narration with Many Children: Usually it's good to start with the youngest child, then work your way up the ages asking if each has anything to add. However, if you use this approach every single time, the older ones might get complacent. ("No, nothing to add.") So you can mix things up a little by calling on any child at random to start the narration sometimes. Not knowing who will be selected to give the oral narration keeps everybody alert and listening. The key is to have one child start the narration and then have the others add to it, not repeat it. That mental exercise of remembering what was already mentioned and searching through your mind for something new to talk about is also a plus!

Written Narration: Older children can be expected to take the next step and write their narrations. If your older child is not used to doing narration, give him several weeks or months to get used to the idea and have some practice narrating orally first. It's harder to keep your train of thought when you have to also think about the mechanics of writing, punctuating, capitalizing, and all such trappings, so make sure your child is adept and successful with organizing and expressing his thoughts orally before adding the writing aspect. Once he is an "old pro" at oral narrations, you can ease him into the written narrations. The lessons in this book will give suggestions for some written narrations. You can determine which of your students can handle those assignments.

Book of Centuries

A Book of Centuries is like a timeline in a notebook. As its name suggests, each two-page spread in the book is devoted to one hundred years—a century—of history. Each student creates his or her own book, recording historical events and names of importance, along with pictures, poems, quotes, and anything else that makes the book individual. You can also add written narrations, illustrations from the Internet, or titles of books you've read that are set in that time period. As they add more history to the book, the students begin to make relations between people who lived in the same era. Most entries will come from history lessons, but the artists, composers, and poets studied in this book will add opportunities for even more connections.

We recommend each student in grades 7–12 create his own Book of Centuries. If your students are not yet old enough to take on the responsibility of their own Books of Centuries, you could create one together as a family. Watch for helpful dates in the timeline column throughout the lessons in this book.

Books of Centuries can be as simple or elaborate as you desire. You can download a free Book of Centuries template at simplycm.com/BOC or purchase a pre-printed, more detailed one in the Simply Charlotte Mason online bookstore.

Habit Training

Habits form character; therefore, one of the most important jobs you have as a parent and an educator is to instill good habits in your children. Success in cultivating good habits depends on two things: repetition and motivation.

Notes

Look through the list of habits in *Laying Down the Rails* and choose one to be your focus for six to eight weeks. Every day look for opportunities to practice doing the good habit you are trying to instill. That constant repetition will help get the new habit firmly embedded. Once or twice a week gather everyone together and read a lesson in *Laying Down the Rails for Children.* (The lesson plans in this book will give you a reminder twice a week. You can adjust that frequency based on how many lessons are provided for the habit you selected and which ones you want to include.) The Scripture passages, stories, poems, and quotes in *Laying Down the Rails for Children* are designed to keep everyone focused on the same goal and motivated toward cultivating that habit.

For more on habit training, download the free e-book, *Smooth and Easy Days*, at simplycm.com/habits.

Short Lessons

Most subjects included in these lesson plans take twenty minutes or less to complete. Short lessons help students cultivate the habit of full attention. You can accomplish much in a short amount of time if everyone is paying attention. You can also accomplish much by doing a little bit regularly. Frequent small portions can add up to a considerable amount.

Wide Variety

Charlotte Mason believed in giving children a wide variety of subjects. Variety keeps the day's work enjoyable, which makes it easier to pay full attention. Providing a broad curriculum also insures that the students receive a balanced education and are introduced to many different ideas. They are respected as individual persons and given opportunities to explore and discover any natural talents or interests outside the three *R*'s. Their minds and hearts are nourished with beauty and their tastes are cultivated toward what is worthy.

On a practical level, a wide variety of subjects provides the teacher with many tools for planning the day's schedule of work. By alternating book-heavy subjects (such as history, literature, science, Bible) with non-book subjects (such a music, art, nature, memory work, handicrafts), the students enjoy using different parts of their brains and do not over-fatigue one part. Be sure to use this principle to your (and your students') advantage. Each day's assignments can be completed in any order and at any times of the day.

Suggestions toward Calculating Credits

Keeping track of high school credits is always a challenge but not that hard once you get the hang of it. You can calculate the credits based on actual time spent interacting with the material, or you can calculate credits based on the amount of work involved. Most authorities agree that if you are calculating based on actual time spent, a credit is awarded for every 120–180 hours spent on task, with 150 being average.

For the completion of assignments in *Enrichment Studies, Volume 1*, I suggest that students should be awarded **1/4 credit for Fine Arts** and **1/2 credit for Literature.**

Below are details demonstrating how the credit suggestions for this study were calculated. The calculations for Hours Spent are an estimated average. The calculations below for the Course Work Detail assume the student completed all the readings and assignments for older students given in these lesson plans.

Hours Spent

Fine Arts—1/4 Credit *(If you continue similar Enrichment studies through all four years of high school, the student will earn 1 full credit of Fine Arts.)*

- Music Study, 10 min. per week x 36 weeks = 6 hours
- Picture Study, 10 min. per week x 36 weeks = 6 hours
- Art Instruction & Handicrafts, 20 min. per week x 36 weeks = 12 hours
- Hymn Study, 10 min. per week x 36 weeks = 6 hours
  Total = 30 hours

Literature—1/2 Credit

- Shakespeare, 20 min. per week x 12 weeks = 4 hours
- Poetry, 10 min. per week x 36 weeks = 6 hours
- Literature Books, 100 min. per week x 36 weeks = 60 hours
  Total = 70 hours

Course Work Detail

Fine Arts

- 3 composers and 24 of their works studied
- 3 artists and 24 of their works studied
- 1 art project completed
- 10 handicraft projects completed
- 6 hymns learned

Literature

- 1 Shakespeare play studied
- 1 poet and 24 of his poems studied
- 3 poems memorized and recited
- 2190 pages read in 6 books (Older Group of books)